Trees and Woody Vines of MISSOURI
Field Guide

Dedication

This book is dedicated to those who appreciate and want to learn more about our native shrubs and woody vines.

Photos by Don Kurz
Back cover photo by Cliff White

On the cover: Buttonbush

Disclaimer: Medicinal or edible uses for plants described in this book are for informational purposes only and should not be read as promotions for medical or herbal prescriptions for self-healing.

Copyright © 2009, 2015, 2017 by the Conservation Commission of the State of Missouri

ISBN 978-1-887247-69-6

Missouri Department of Conservation
P.O. Box 180
Jefferson City, MO 65102-0180
mdc.mo.gov

Equal opportunity to participate in and benefit from programs of the Missouri Department of Conservation is available to all individuals without regard to their race, color, religion, national origin, sex, ancestry, age, sexual orientation, veteran status, or disability. Questions should be directed to the Department of Conservation, PO Box 180, Jefferson City, MO 65102, 573-751-4115 (voice) or 800-735-2966 (TTY), or to Chief, Public Civil Rights, Office of Civil Rights, U.S. Department of the Interior, 1849 C Street, NW, Washington, D.C. 20240.

Shrubs and Woody Vines of MISSOURI
Field Guide

by Don Kurz

illustrations by Paul Nelson
colorization by Diana Jayne

Serving nature and you

Missouri Department of Conservation

Acknowledgments

The beautiful illustrations are provided by Paul Nelson, an outstanding botanical illustrator. His keen eye for detail and his technique of capturing a plant's growth habit by drawing from fresh material adds special three-dimensional qualities to his work. Diana Jayne then added beautiful color enhancements to Paul's black-and-white illustrations. Appreciation also goes to botanist Tim Smith for reviewing the shrub and woody-vine descriptions, and to Karen Hudson, marketing specialist, and Bernadette Dryden, publications supervisor, for their support of the project. And thanks to Marci Porter, designer extraordinaire, for her crafting of an attractive final product similar to her creation of the *Trees of Missouri Field Guide*.

Snow wreath

It is a wholesome and necessary thing for us to turn again to the earth and in the contemplation of her beauties to know of wonder and humility.

—Rachel Carson

Contents

Introduction 3

How to use this book 5

Map of Missouri 7

Leaf arrangements and shapes 8

Shrubs 10

    Leaves opposite, simple 12
        Dogwoods, swamp privet, viburnums,
        fringe tree, buttonbush, euonymus, buckbrush,
        wolfberry, American hydrangea, beautyberry,
        mock orange, St. John's-wort, St. Andrew's cross,
        American Christmas mistletoe, common buckthorn,
        border privet, bush honeysuckle

    Leaves opposite, compound 32
        Buckeyes, elderberries, American bladdernut,
        false indigo, lead plant

    Leaves alternate, simple 38
        Crab apples, wild plums, choke cherry, peach,
        perfumed cherry, black chokeberry, willows,
        meadowsweet, hardhack, wild blueberries,
        black huckleberry, hollies, water elm,
        buckthorns, leatherwood, hawthorns, snow
        wreath, alder, barberries, musclewood, hop
        hornbeam, hazelnut, gooseberries, American
        black currant, golden currant, spice bush,
        pondberry, witch-hazels, wild azalea, snowbell,
        corkwood, Virginia willow, New Jersey tea,
        redroot, buckbrush, eastern redbud, service berry,
        alternate-leaved dogwood, dwarf chestnut oak,
        dwarf hackberry, American smoke tree, jointweed,
        ninebark, staggerbush, autumn olive, matrimony
        vine, rose of Sharon, yuccas, giant cane, pawpaw

Leaves alternate, compound 88
   Roses, prickly ash, bristly locust, sumacs,
   blackberries, raspberry, dewberries, Eastern poison
   oak, hop tree, prairie acacia, devil's walking stick

Woody Vines.. 108

   Leaves opposite, simple... 110
      Honeysuckles, climbing dogbane, partridge
      berry, common periwinkle, wintercreeper

   Leaves opposite, compound 118
      Cross vine, trumpet creeper, virgin's bower

   Leaves alternate, simple.. 122
      Grapes, supple-jack, woolly pipevine,
      catbriers, ladies' eardrops, bittersweets,
      moonseeds, cupseed

   Leaves alternate, compound 138
      Virginia creeper, woodbine, pepper vine,
      poison ivy, marine vine, wisteria

**Non-native shrubs and woody vines
   naturalized in Missouri**... 144

Index... 145

Wild azalea

Introduction

This is a field guide to the identification of shrubs and vines occurring in Missouri that are either native to the state or have become naturalized by reproducing on their own. Small trees can sometimes be mistaken for large shrubs, so they are also included. A tree, as defined by the American Forestry Association, is a woody plant with a single stem or trunk at least 3 inches in diameter at breast height (4½ feet above ground). A tree is also at least 13 feet tall at maturity, with a definite crown of foliage. In comparison, a shrub has multiple stems arising from the ground and is generally smaller than a tree. Woody vines have stems that require support, either by creeping along the ground or climbing by way of tendrils (slender twining appendages) or by other means such as the coiling of their stems. (For more information about trees, shrubs and woody vines, refer to *Trees of Missouri* and *Shrubs and Woody Vines of Missouri*, both Missouri Department of Conservation publications.)

Some plants that are considered woody farther south die back to the ground in Missouri and states farther north due to colder winter temperatures. Only plants that retain some woody tissue above or at ground level are included here. Shrubs and woody vines classified as rare or endangered or thought to be eliminated from the flora of the state are also described and illustrated, with the hope that new locations will be found.

There are 128 native shrubs and 33 native woody vines in Missouri. For the purpose of discussion in this field guide, a native shrub or woody vine is one that occurred in Missouri prior to the arrival of European settlers. These are shrubs and woody vines that are well adapted to living and reproducing in the same soil, topography and climate for thousands of years. Also, wildlife has evolved to depend on selected types of shrubs and woody vines for food and cover. In contrast, a naturalized shrub or woody vine, often referred to as non-native, exotic or alien, is one that has "escaped" into a new habitat due to human influence.

Many of these non-native shrubs and woody vines spread from their original plantings and invade nearby natural communities, often spreading prolifically and reducing the diversity of the natural community. These exotic plant species are so successful because the herbivores that kept their growth in check in their original homeland did not make the journey with them to their new environment. These non-native shrubs (such as autumn olive) and woody vines (such as Japanese honeysuckle) often become a nuisance, with eradication proving costly and time-consuming. Described in this book are 18 species of shrubs and 8 species of woody vines with origins primarily in Europe and Asia that have naturalized in the state. These exotic species disrupt the natural balance of Missouri's forests, savannas and woodlands, and planting these species that are known to be invasive is discouraged. A list of the non-native shrubs and non-native woody vines is provided on page 144.

Trumpet honeysuckle

How to use this book

Leaves
This field guide is designed to identify shrubs and woody vines primarily by the arrangement and shape of their leaves. To help in recognizing the difference between simple and compound leaves, remember that a simple leaf is undivided but a compound leaf can have two or more distinct leaflets. A compound leaf has a central stalk that resembles a stem and the leaflets may look like simple leaves. However, there is always a bud (next year's growth) in the axil of a leaf (the angle between the leaf and the stem). There is never a bud in the axil of a leaflet.

Since leaves are found either on or beneath the shrubs and woody vines year round, their identifying characteristics are more reliable than bark, which changes as the plant ages, winter twigs, which cannot always be reached, or fruit and flowers, which often appear for only a few weeks or months of the year.

The illustrations on pages 8–9 show the types of leaf arrangements and shapes referred to in the plant descriptions throughout the book.

Plant names
Common names for plants are easy to learn, but they sometimes lead to confusion and misunderstanding; one species may have several names, and one name can sometimes be applied to more than one plant. Common names are frequently local and vary from place to place, but there is only one scientific name, and that name is used worldwide.

Scientific names are in Latin form, and their construction and use are governed by the International Code of Botanical Nomenclature, a detailed set of rules adopted by systematic botanists. Scientific names are binomial (two-named), composed of a genus name followed by the species name. The genus name is a noun, sometimes commemorating a noted botanist, or is simply the classical name for the group. The first letter of the genus is always capitalized and is always set in italics; an example is *Cornus*, the name for the dogwoods. The species name is an adjective, modifying the noun, and it is always written in lowercase letters and also italicized. An example is *florida*, which means "flowering" and can refer to large flowers. Therefore, the scientific name for flowering dogwood is *Cornus florida*. The derivation of the scientific name and common name for every shrub and woody vine in this book can be found in the more detailed *Shrubs and Woody Vines of Missouri*, published by the Missouri Department of Conservation.

Descriptions

Every illustration is accompanied with information on distinguishing characteristics that aid in identifying the shrub or woody vine. The general size and shape of the species are given. The leaves are described by their position, shape, length, width, margins, upper surface, lower surface and color. The flower description includes the color, reproductive type, arrangement on the stem, length, width and fragrance. Fruit information may include type, texture, color and other features such as edibility.

Moonseed

The habitat refers to the natural location where the shrub or woody vine is likely to be found living and reproducing. Information is also provided on whether the tree is native to the state.

A map for each shrub or woody vine's natural range within the state shows where one might expect to find a particular plant. There are no shrub or woody vine species in Missouri that are found exclusively within its borders. In all cases, they extend their range into other states and even regions. Non-native shrubs and woody vines do not have a natural range within the state and can be planted anywhere, so the statement "escapes from cultivation" or some similar description is given.

State of
MISSOURI

Beautyberry

Trumpet honeysuckle

Leaf arrangements and shapes

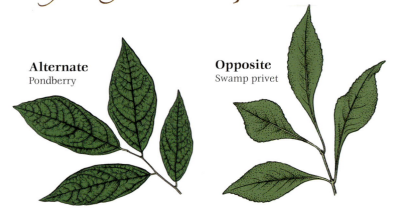

Alternate
Pondberry

Opposite
Swamp privet

Simple
Hortulan plum

Compound
Prairie wild rose

Smooth margin
Swamp dogwood

Toothed margin
Wild plum

Wavy margin
Eastern witch-hazel

Shallow lobes
Frosty hawthorn

Deep lobes
Cupseed

Broadest below the middle
Water elm

Broadest above the middle
Alder

Triangular
Raccoon grape

Lance-shaped
Carolina willow

Heart-shaped
Eastern redbud

Palm-shaped
Red buckeye

Strawberry bush

Golden currant

Ninebark

Hardhack

Shrubs

Pasture rose

OPPOSITE, SIMPLE

OPPOSITE, COMPOUND

ALTERNATE, SIMPLE

ALTERNATE, COMPOUND

LEAVES OPPOSITE, SIMPLE

DOGWOODS

Flowering dogwood *(Cornus florida)*

A shrub to small tree up to 40 feet tall, with a straggling, spreading crown. Leaves opposite, simple, 3 to 5 inches long, 1½ to 2½ inches wide; margins lacking teeth; deeply veined. Flowers with 4 white modified leaves (bracts), each 1½ to 2½ inches long, notched at the tip and surrounding a cluster of 25 to 30 small, yellowish flowers. Berries in clusters, shiny, red, ¼ to ½ inch long. Found along wooded slopes, ravines, along bluffs, upland ridges and old fields. Missouri's official state tree, it flowers in April shortly after—but sometimes overlapping with—eastern redbud.

Rough-leaved dogwood *(Cornus drummondii)*

Irregularly branched shrub or small spreading tree, rarely up to 30 feet tall. Leaves opposite, simple, 1 to 5 inches long, ½ to 2½ inches wide, longer than broad to widest in the middle; margins lacking teeth; rough-hairy above, woolly below. Flowers whitish in spreading clusters, 1 to 3 inches across, with 4 spreading petals. Berries white, about ¼ inch across. Occurs in dry or rocky woods, thickets, old fields, limestone and dolomite glades, prairies, and along ponds and streams. It spreads by underground stems, sending up sprouts at the margin of the thicket.

Swamp dogwood, silky dogwood

(Cornus amomum ssp. *obliqua)*
An open, irregularly branched shrub up to 9 feet tall, rarely taking on the appearance of a small tree. Leaves opposite, simple, 1½ to 3¼ inches long, ½ to 1½ inches wide, longer than broad; lacking teeth along the margins; lower surface whitish and smooth or with flattened hairs. Flowers white, in flat or sometimes indented clusters, each flower with 4 small petals. Berries blue, about ¼ inch in diameter, often with a style (small stalk) at the tip. Occurs in and along rocky banks of streams, spring branches, wet places in prairies, fens, wet thickets, swamps, low woodlands and margins of ponds. Also known as *Cornus obliqua*.

Flowering dogwood

Rough-leaved dogwood

Swamp dogwood, silky dogwood

DOGWOODS CONT'D, SWAMP PRIVET

Stiff dogwood *(Cornus foemina)*
A shrub with stiff, upright, irregular branches; sometimes a small tree up to 15 feet tall. Leaves opposite, simple, 1 to 3 inches long, 1 to 1¾ inches wide, widest at the middle; smooth along the margins; lower surface slightly paler and lacking hairs. Flowers white, in clusters 1¼ to 2 inches broad, each flower with 4 small petals. Berries pale blue, about ¼ inch across. Occurs along edges of swamps and in low wet woodlands and wet open ground in the lowland counties of southeastern Missouri. Also known as *Cornus foemina* ssp. *foemina*.

Gray dogwood *(Cornus racemosa)*
A thicket-forming shrub up to 12 feet tall; occasionally a small tree. Leaves opposite, simple, 1 to 4 inches long, ½ to 1½ inches wide, widest at the middle; smooth along the margins and upper surface, hairy beneath. Flowers white, in branching clusters, 1¼ to 2½ inches high or broad, with the stalk below the flower cluster conspicuously red; petals 4, each about ⅛ inch long. Berries white, resembling a depressed globe, about ¼ inch in diameter. Occurs in moist or rocky soils along streams and ponds, and in glades, prairies and thickets along fencerows and roadsides. Also known as *Cornus foemina* ssp. *racemosa*.

Swamp privet *(Forestiera acuminata)*
A straggly shrub or small tree up to 30 feet tall. Leaves opposite, simple, 2 to 4½ inches long, 1 to 2 inches wide, broadest at the middle with base narrowly wedge-shaped; margins with few teeth; yellowish-green above, paler, with occasional hairs on veins beneath. Flowers yellow, in dense clusters, appearing before leaves; male and female flowers on separate plants; petals lacking. Fruit purplish, sometimes curved, about 1 inch long. Occurs in swamps; low wet woods; and borders of streams, ponds, sloughs and bayous. In Missouri mainly along the Mississippi River and in the Bootheel.

Stiff dogwood

Gray dogwood

Swamp privet

OPPOSITE, SIMPLE

VIBURNUMS

Southern blackhaw, rusty blackhaw
(Viburnum rufidulum)
An irregularly branched shrub to small tree up to 18 feet tall. Leaves opposite, simple, 1½ to 4 inches long, 1 to 2½ inches wide, broadest at or above the middle, leathery; margins finely toothed; upper surface glossy; lower surface paler, with scattered, rust-colored hairs that are also found on leaf stalks. Flowers white, in flat clusters 2 to 6 inches across, numerous; each flower about ¼ inch across with 5 petals. Fruit bluish-black, about ⅜ inch long, in drooping clusters; stalks red. Occurs in rocky or dry woods; rich, moist valleys; and alluvial ground along streams, rocky glades and thickets.

Blackhaw *(Viburnum prunifolium)*
A shrub or small tree up to 18 feet tall, with stiff, spreading branches forming an irregular crown near the top. Leaves opposite, simple, 1½ to 3 inches long, 1 to 1¾ inches wide, thin, egg-shaped; margins finely toothed; upper surface dull green, not shiny, lacking hairs. Flowers white, in round-topped clusters 2 to 4 inches across, numerous; petals 5. Fruit bluish-black with a white coating, about ½ inch long; stalks red. Occurs in low woods along streams, at the bases and edges of bluffs, in dry upper slopes of ravines and in thickets.

Downy arrowwood *(Viburnum rafinesquianum)*
A rather loose, straggly shrub up to 6 feet tall. Leaves opposite, simple, 1 to 3 inches long, 1¼ to 2 inches wide, broadest at or below the middle with the base heart-shaped; margins coarsely toothed with 4 to 10 teeth along each side of the leaf blade; upper surface dull green and smooth; lower surface densely hairy. Flowers white, in clusters on the ends of branches, clusters ¾ to 2½ inches across; flowers numerous, each about ¼ inch across; petals 5. Fruit dark purple, glossy, about ¼ inch across; globe-shaped. Occurs on steep wooded bluffs and in rocky open woods, generally bordering streams.

VIBURNUMS CONT'D

Softleaf arrowwood *(Viburnum molle)*
A shrub 9 to 12 feet tall, with gray, shredding bark. Leaves opposite, simple, 2 to 5 inches long and about as wide, round to egg-shaped, base deeply heart-shaped; margins coarsely toothed, usually 16 to 30 teeth along each side of the leaf blade; upper surface dark green, smooth to slightly hairy; lower surface pale and soft-hairy. Flowers white, in clusters 2 to 3½ inches across; flowers numerous, about ¼ inch across; petals 5. Fruit bluish-black, about ⅜ inch long, flattened. Occurs on steep wooded slopes above and below bluffs, on talus slopes, and in rocky woods along streams. A closely related viburnum, Ozark arrowwood, *Viburnum ozarkense*, differs by having a hairy upper leaf surface, a hairy leaf stalk and tight bark; it is known only in Missouri from Howell and Oregon counties.

Southern arrowwood *(Viburnum dentatum)*
A shrub attaining a height of up to 15 feet, with slender, elongate, ascending branches. Leaves opposite, simple, 1 to 4½ inches long and wide, circular to broadly egg-shaped, base rounded to nearly heart-shaped; margins with teeth pointed to rounded; upper surface smooth or nearly so or with star-shaped hairs; lower surface with star-shaped hairs. Flowers white, in clusters 1¼ to 4½ inches across; flowers small, numerous, with five spreading petals. Fruit bluish-black, about ¼ inch across. Occurs in low alluvial woods on terraces and wooded slopes. Endangered in Missouri.

Northern arrowwood *(Viburnum recognitum)*
A shrub attaining a height of up to 16 feet, with slender, elongate, ascending branches. Leaves opposite, simple, 1 to 4½ inches long and wide, circular to broadly egg-shaped, base blunt or rounded or nearly heart-shaped; margins with teeth pointed to rounded; upper surface smooth; lower surface smooth with some hairs along the veins. Flowers white, in clusters 1¼ to 4½ inches broad; flowers small, numerous with 5 spreading petals. Fruit bluish-black, about ¼ inch across. Occurs along gravel bars of small streams. Endangered in Missouri.

VIBURNUMS CONT'D, FRINGE TREE, BUTTONBUSH

Nannyberry *(Viburnum lentago)*
A shrub up to 18 feet tall, often in small, open colonies. Leaves opposite, simple, 2¼ to 3 inches long, 1 to 1½ inches wide, broadest at the middle, tip abruptly slender and long-pointed, base wedge-shaped to rounded with the leaf stalk winged or wavy; margins finely toothed; upper surface dark green; lower surface slightly paler, with reddish, star-shaped hairs. Flowers white, in round-topped clusters, 2 to 5 inches across; flowers small, numerous, with 5 spreading petals. Fruit dark blue, about ⅜ inch long, often in drooping clusters. Occurs in low woods, on wooded slopes and in moist valleys bordering or near streams. Endangered in Missouri.

Fringe tree *(Chionanthus virginicus)*
Usually a shrub with crooked branches, but sometimes a tree up to 35 feet tall. Leaves opposite, simple, may appear whorled near the tips of the twigs, large, 4 to 8 inches long, 1 to 4 inches wide, oval to egg-shaped or lance-shaped; margins often wavy, lacking teeth; upper surface dark green, smooth; lower surface paler, with hairs on the veins. Flowers white with purple spots near the base, occurring in delicate drooping bundles along the twig at the leaf attachment; petals 4 to 6, narrow, about 1 inch long; fragrant. Fruit bluish-black, ½ to ¾ inch long, in clusters. Occurs along rocky, wooded dolomite ledges and bluffs and along the edges of dolomite glades in southwest Missouri and in low wet woods in southeast Missouri.

Buttonbush *(Cephalanthus occidentalis)*
A shrub or small tree up to 18 feet tall, growing in low areas, often swollen at the base. Leaves opposite, but more commonly in whorls of 3, simple, blades 2 to 8 inches long, 1 to 3 inches wide, oval or lance-shaped; margins lacking teeth; upper surface dark green, smooth; lower surface paler, with a few hairs along the veins. Flowers white, fragrant, numerous, clustered in globe-shaped heads 1 to 1½ inches in diameter; flowers small, with 4 short, spreading lobes and long stamens. Fruit a round cluster of reddish-brown nutlets. Occurs in low wet woods, swamps and thickets, borders of streams and sloughs, upland sinkhole ponds, and river-bottom oxbow lakes and ponds.

Nannyberry

Fringe tree

Buttonbush

EUONYMUS

Wahoo *(Euonymus atropurpureus)*
Usually a shrub, but sometimes a small tree up to 25 feet tall, with spreading branches and an irregular crown. Twigs 4-angled, purplish-green when young, turning brownish later. Leaves opposite, simple, 2 to 5 inches long, 1 to 2 inches wide, broadest at the middle; margins finely toothed; bright green above; pale and hairy beneath. Flowers purple, about ½ inch across, in clusters of 7 to 15 on drooping stalks; petals 4. Fruit purple to rose-colored, deeply 4-lobed, persistent into winter on long stalks, splitting open to expose a scarlet seed covering. Occurs on wooded slopes and bluffs, in open woods, along streams and in thickets.

Burning bush, winged euonymus
(Euonymus alatus)
A shrub growing to a height of 15 to 20 feet, with corky wings on the twigs. Leaves opposite, simple, 1 to 3 inches long, ½ to 1¼ inches wide, broadest at the middle, base wedge-shaped; margins finely and sharply toothed; upper surface medium to dark green; lower surface paler, smooth to somewhat hairy. Flowers yellowish-green, about ½ inch across, in clusters of 3 to 8; petals 4 with wavy margins. Fruit deeply 4-lobed, about ¼ inch long, red, splitting open to expose an orange to red seed coating. Introduced from Asia and used for yard decoration because of its brilliant red foliage in autumn; sometimes escapes into nearby open woods.

Strawberry bush *(Euonymus americanus)*
A shrub to 6 feet tall, sometimes creeping or trailing. Leaves opposite, simple, ¾ to 4 inches long, ½ to 1 inch wide, broadest at the middle to lower half, base rounded; margins toothed; upper surface smooth and dark green; lower surface smooth or slightly hairy on the veins. Flowers greenish to greenish-purple or reddish, about ¼ to ½ inch across, in clusters of 1 to 3, with 5 petals. Fruit pink, about ½ inch across, globe-shaped and flattened at the base with a warty surface, spitting to expose up to five orange-red seeds. Occurs in low sandy woods along spring branches, low moist woods and moist stream banks. Rare in Missouri.

Wahoo

Burning bush, winged euonymus

Strawberry bush

OPPOSITE, SIMPLE

EUONYMUS CONT'D, BUCKBRUSH, WOLFBERRY

Running strawberry bush
(Euonymus obovatus)
A very small shrub, less than 18 inches tall, with trailing stems up to 3 feet long. Twigs bright green to purple with broad ridges or angles and rooting when in contact with the ground. Leaves opposite, simple, 1 to 2½ inches long, ¾ to 1¾ inches wide, broadest at or above the middle at the upper end of twigs, base wedge-shaped; margins finely toothed; upper surface medium to dark green; lower surface paler and smooth. Flowers greenish to purple, about ½ inch across, in clusters of 1 to 3; petals 5. Fruit pale orange to scarlet red, about ¾ inch across with a warty surface, splitting to expose 1 to 2 scarlet seeds. Occurs on mostly north-facing, moist, wooded dolomite slopes or at the bases of dolomite bluffs.

Buckbrush, coral berry
(Symphoricarpos orbiculatus)
A thicket-forming shrub up to 4 feet tall, with single trailing stems when young. Leaves opposite, simple, 1½ to 2 inches long, ½ to 1½ inches wide, broadest below the middle to oval; margins smooth, sometimes with a few large, rounded teeth; upper surface dull green, smooth; lower surface paler, smooth to hairy. Flowers greenish-white, sometimes purplish, about ⅛ inch long, bell-shaped with 5 petals. Fruit pink to coral-red, persistent in winter, in dense clusters, globe-shaped, about ¼ inch across. Occurs in grazed and second-growth dry or rocky woodlands, old fields, pastures and thickets; on rocky bluffs; and along railroads.

Wolfberry *(Symphoricarpos occidentalis)*
A shrub 1 to 4 feet tall, with shoots arising from the roots and forming thickets. Leaves opposite, simple, 1 to 4½ inches long, ¾ to 2¾ inches wide, oval to broadest below the middle, base wedge-shaped or rounded; margins smooth or with coarse round teeth; upper surface dull, yellowish-green or grayish-green; lower surface grayish-green, sometimes with fine hairs. Flowers white or pink, about ¼ inch long, hairy inside, in clusters of 10 to 20; petals 5. Fruit white, persistent in winter, in dense clusters, globe-shaped, about ¼ inch across. Occurs on loess hills along woods and prairies, on open banks and in thickets. Endangered in Missouri.

Running strawberry bush

OPPOSITE, SIMPLE

Buckbrush, coral berry

Wolfberry

AMERICAN HYDRANGEA, BEAUTYBERRY, MOCK ORANGE

American hydrangea *(Hydrangea arborescens)*
A wide-branching, straggly shrub growing in
clumps and attaining a height of 2 to 6 feet. Leaves
opposite, simple, 2 to 6 inches long, 3 to 5 inches
wide, broadest at the middle to circular, base
heart-shaped or rounded; margins sharply toothed; upper surface
dark green, smooth; lower surface paler and somewhat hairy.
Flowers white, minute, in clusters 2 to 6 inches across, with the
flowers along the margin much larger and often sterile. Fruit are
small capsules about ⅛ inch long and wide, with 8 to 10 ribs along
the sides and 2 horns at the tip. Occurs in moist or rocky wooded
slopes, on talus, at the bases of bluffs, along streams and in ravines.

OPPOSITE, SIMPLE

Beautyberry, French mulberry
(Callicarpa americana)
A many-branched shrub to 9 feet tall. Leaves
opposite, simple, aromatic, 3 to 9 inches long, 1½ to
5 inches wide, broadest at or above the middle, base
wedge-shaped; margins coarsely toothed; upper surface dark green,
smooth or powdery; lower surface paler, with dense, star-shaped
hairs. Flowers rose to pink or pale blue, in clusters arising from the
leaf axils; petals 4-lobed. Fruit rose to purple or violet to blue, in
dense clusters in leaf axils, globe-shaped, ⅛ to ¼ inch long. Occurs
on wooded dolomite slopes bordering the White River and in one
site in Ripley County. Endangered in Missouri. There are Asian
species planted as ornamentals that differ mainly by having the
fruit on 1-inch stalks arising from the leaf axils.

Mock orange *(Philadelphus pubescens)*
A vigorous shrub 3 to 15 feet tall, with gray bark
shredding into thin, narrow strips. Leaves opposite,
simple, 2 to 3¼ inches long, about 1 inch wide,
widest in the middle; margins smooth or sharply
and randomly toothed; upper surface dark green, smooth; lower
surface pale with gray hairs. Flowers white, 1 to 1½ inches across
in clusters of 5 to 9 flowers; petals 4. Fruit a capsule, splitting at
the top with numerous small seeds. Occurs on north-facing, steep,
wooded bluffs and slopes. Endangered in Missouri. A similar
species, sweet mock orange (*Philadelphus coronarius*), is from
Europe and differs by having brown bark. The native mock
orange has gray bark.

American hydrangea

Beautyberry, French mulberry

Mock orange

OPPOSITE, SIMPLE

ST. JOHN'S-WORT, ST. ANDREW'S CROSS, MISTLETOE

Shrubby St. John's-wort *(Hypericum prolificum)*
A shrub 1 to 6 feet tall, usually many-branched above the base. Leaves opposite, simple, 1 to 3 inches long, ¼ to ½ inch wide, narrow throughout to slightly broader in the middle, the base narrowed into a short, often winged stalk; margins lacking teeth, slightly curved under; upper surface dull green; lower paler. Flowers bright yellow, ¾ to 1 inch across, often paired; petals 5 with numerous stamens. Fruit a capsule, about ¾ inch long, splitting at the tip with numerous small seeds. Occurs in rocky ground and gravel bars along streams, on dry wooded slopes and in old fields. Also known as *Hypericum spathulatum*. Another St. John's-wort, *Hypericum lobocarpum*, has been reported from Dunklin and Howell counties. It has winged stems, more flowers in clusters, and a smaller seed capsule (about ¼ inch long).

St. Andrew's cross *(Hypericum hypericoides)*
A small, sprawling shrub ½ to 3 feet tall. Leaves opposite, simple, evergreen, ½ to 1½ inches long, about ¼ inch wide, base narrowed; margins smooth; upper surface bright green, smooth, with dotted small spots or glands; lower surface paler, smooth. Flowers bright yellow, about ½ to ¾ inch wide, often solitary; petals 4, arranged in a cross. Fruit a capsule, about ⅜ inch long, flattened, splitting into two sides releasing numerous small seeds. Occurs in dry, rocky, open woods on upland slopes and ridges, or in wooded valleys and ravines, in acid soils associated with chert, sandstone or igneous-base soils. Formerly known as *Ascyrum hypericoides*.

American Christmas mistletoe
(Phoradendron leucarpum)
A small shrub up to 2 feet tall, semiparasitic on branches of deciduous trees. Leaves opposite, simple, 1 to 2 inches long, ⅜ to ¾ inch wide, broadest at or above the middle, base tapering; margins lacking teeth; both surfaces dark green to yellowish-green, smooth, leathery. Flowers green, in clusters of 2 to 3 along a spike ⅜ to 2 inches long; petals lacking. Fruit white or creamy, about ¼ inch long, translucent, globe-shaped and flattened at the base, sticky when crushed. Occurs in low woods in valleys and along streams, where it is commonly found on sycamore trees. In the lowlands of the Bootheel, it can be found on black gum and river birch.

Shrubby St. John's-wort

OPPOSITE, SIMPLE

St. Andrew's cross

American Christmas mistletoe

COMMON BUCKTHORN, BORDER PRIVET, BUSH HONEYSUCKLE

Common buckthorn *(Rhamnus cathartica)*
A profusely branched shrub or small tree up to 25 feet tall. Twigs often ending in a thorn. Leaves mostly opposite, simple, 1¼ to 3 inches long, 1 to 2¼ inches wide, lance-shaped to broadest at or above the middle, base tapering, tip abruptly pointed; margins toothed with tips usually turned in and bearing a gland; upper surface dark green, smooth; lower surface paler, smooth. Flowers green to yellowish-green, on stalks in clusters of 2 to 6 for male flowers and up to 15 for female flowers; petals 4 when present. Fruit black, globe-shaped, ¼ to ⅜ inch across, somewhat glossy. Introduced from Europe; escapes from cultivation into woodlands and tallgrass prairie.

Border privet *(Ligustrum obtusifolium)*
A vigorous shrub forming a dense thicket to a height of 15 feet. Leaves opposite, simple, 1 to 2½ inches long, ¼ to 1 inch wide, broadest in the middle and tapering at both ends, base wedge-shaped to rounded; margins lacking teeth; upper surface medium green, smooth; lower surface paler, hairy, at least on the midvein. Flowers dull white, tubular, in clusters of 2 to 10; petals 4. Fruit black, about ⅛ inch long, globe-shaped, in clusters of 2 to 6. Introduced from Japan; spreads into edges of woods and disturbed sites. There are other species of non-native privet also found in Missouri.

Bush honeysuckle *(Lonicera maackii)*
A large, upright, spreading shrub up to 15 feet in height. Leaves opposite, simple, 2 to 3 inches long, ½ to 1½ inches wide, broadest at or above the middle, with both ends tapering; margins fringed with fine hairs, teeth lacking; upper surface dark green; lower surface paler, often hairy along the veins. Flowers white changing to yellow, about 1 inch long in clusters; petals 2, upper with 4 lobes, lower with 1 lobe. Fruit red, about ¼ inch across. Introduced from Asia; spreads into woodlands, often dominating the understory. Another bush honeysuckle, *Lonicera × bella*, differs by having leaves 1½ to 2 inches long, with both ends rounded and a short point at the tip; the upper surface is blue-green with soft hairs underneath. It also has aggressive traits.

LEAVES OPPOSITE, COMPOUND

BUCKEYES

Ohio buckeye *(Aesculus glabra)*

A shrub to medium-sized tree up to 50 feet tall (depending upon site conditions), branches drooping with up-curved ends. Leaves opposite, palm-shaped, with 5 to 7 leaflets; leaflets 4 to 6 inches long, 1½ to 2½ inches wide, broadest in the middle; margins finely toothed; upper surface bluish- or grass-green; lower surface paler, smooth. Flowers greenish yellow, about ¾ inch long, clustered along an axis 4 to 8 inches long on the tips of twigs; petals 4; stamens longer than the petals. Fruit a light brown, leathery capsule; 1 to 2¼ inches across, globe-shaped, roughened by blunt spines, splitting into 3 parts; seeds 3, brown, shiny. Occurs in rich or rocky woods of valleys, ravines, edges of low woods and thickets.

Red buckeye *(Aesculus pavia)*

A shrub or, more rarely, a small tree up to 20 feet tall, with a somewhat dense crown and short, drooping branches with up-curved ends. Leaves opposite, palm-shaped with 5 leaflets; leaflets 3 to 6 inches long, 1 to 1½ inches wide, broadest at or above the middle; margins coarsely toothed; upper surface shiny, dark green; lower surface paler, with smooth to matted hairs. Flowers red, about 1 inch long, clustered along an axis 4 to 8 inches long on the tips of twigs; petals 4, unequal in length; stamens shorter than or only slightly longer than the upper petals. Fruit a light brown, leathery capsule, 1 to 2 inches across, elongated to globe-shaped, smooth but finely pitted, splitting into 3 parts; seeds 1 to 3, light to dark brown, shiny, about 1 inch across. Occurs in low, rich woods in valleys, on low slopes and along streams

Ohio buckeye

Red buckeye

OPPOSITE, COMPOUND

ELDERBERRIES

Common elderberry *(Sambucus canadensis)*
A shrub to 8 feet tall, forming colonies from root sprouts, with branches occurring near the top. Leaves opposite, compound, 4 to 12 inches long with 5 to 7 leaflets; leaflets 2 to 6 inches long, 1 to 2 inches wide, lance-shaped to sometimes broadest at the middle; margins sharply toothed; upper surface shiny, bright green, smooth; lower surface paler, barely or densely hairy. Flowers white, sweet-scented, about ¼ inch across, in flattened flower clusters sometimes up to 10 inches across at the tip of twigs; petals 5. Fruit purple or black, about ¼ inch across, smooth, glossy, bittersweet. Occurs in open woods and thickets and along streams, fencerows, roadsides and railroads.

Red-berried elderberry *(Sambucus pubens)*
A shrub or small tree up to 24 feet tall, not forming colonies. Leaves opposite, compound, 3 to 7 inches long with 5 to 7 leaflets; leaflets 2 to 4 inches long, ¾ to 1¼ inches wide, broadly lance-shaped to broadest below the middle, blades often with uneven sides; margins sharply toothed; upper surface dark green; lower surface paler, hairy at first, smooth later. Flowers white, about ⅛ inch across, in pyramidal clusters 2 to 4 inches long, 1¼ to 2 inches wide; petals 5. Fruit red, semiglossy, about ⅛ inch across, in pyramidal clusters up to 4 inches long. Occurs on shaded, north- to northeast-facing wooded limestone bluffs and ledges; in Missouri found only in Marion County. Endangered in Missouri. Formerly known as *Sambucus racemosa* ssp. *pubens*.

Common elderberry

Red-berried elderberry

AMERICAN BLADDERNUT, FALSE INDIGO, LEAD PLANT

American bladdernut *(Staphylea trifolia)*

A thicket-forming shrub or small tree up to 25 feet tall, with the branches near the top. Leaves opposite, compound, with 3 leaflets each 1½ to 4 inches long, 1¼ to 2 inches wide, broadest at or below the middle; margins sharply toothed; upper surface bright green, hairy on the veins; lower surface slightly paler, hairy. Flowers white, about ¼ inch long, in drooping clusters on hairy stalks; petals 5; stamens extending beyond the petals. Fruit drooping, in clusters of 2 to 5, persistent until midwinter; capsule bladderlike, 3-lobed; seeds 1 to 4, yellowish to grayish-brown, hard, shiny. Occurs in rich wooded valleys, on north- or east-facing wooded slopes (especially of limestone or dolomite), along streams and in thickets.

False indigo, indigo bush *(Amorpha fruticosa)*
A shrub often clumped, branching to 12 feet high. Leaves opposite, compound, 2½ to 10 inches long; leaflets 9 to 27, ¾ to 1½ inches long, ⅜ to ¾ inch wide, oval to longer than broad, tip rounded to abruptly pointed, base rounded or wedge-shaped; margins lacking teeth; upper surface dull green and smooth; lower surface paler and smooth or finely hairy. Flowers purplish-blue, ¼ inch long, in dense clusters 2½ to 6 inches long; petals forming a tube, with the tips lobed. Fruit a pod, ¼ to ⅜ inch long, smooth with resinous dots. Occurs in moist ground in thickets along streams, rocky banks, borders of ponds and low, open, wet woods.

Lead plant *(Amorpha canescens)*
An erect or ascending shrub 1 to 3 feet, leafy to the base. Leaves opposite, compound, 1½ to 5 inches long, each dissected leaf with 13 to 49 leaflets; leaflets small, less than ¾ inch long, widest in the middle or below, tip and base rounded; margins lacking teeth; upper surface gray-green with flattened hairs; lower surface paler, with gray hairs. Flowers bluish-purple, ¼ inch long, in dense clusters up to 10 inches long; petals tubular with the tip lobed. Fruit a pod, ⅛ to ¼ inch long, densely hairy. Occurs in prairies, glades and woodlands.

American bladdernut

False indigo, indigo bush

Lead plant

OPPOSITE, COMPOUND

LEAVES ALTERNATE, SIMPLE

CRAB APPLES

Narrow-leaved crab apple *(Malus angustifolia)*
A large, thorny shrub to small tree up to 26 feet tall, forming a broad, open crown; sometimes thicket-forming with rigid, thorny branches. Leaves alternate, simple, leathery, 1 to 3 inches long, ½ to 2 inches wide, narrow, broadest at the middle; margins with rounded teeth; upper surface dull green; lower surface occasionally with hairs along the veins. Flowers white to pink, about 1 inch across, in clusters of 3 to 5; petals 5, narrowing at the base; fragrant. Fruit pale yellowish-green, ¾ to 1 inch across, globe-shaped, fleshy, sour. Occurs in sandy soils in the southeastern Missouri Bootheel. Rare in Missouri.

Sweet crab apple *(Malus coronaria)*
A large, thorny shrub to small, bushy tree up to 26 feet tall, stiffly branched, with a broadly rounded crown. Leaves alternate, simple, 1¼ to 3 inches long, ½ to 1½ inches wide, broadest below the middle to somewhat triangular; margins occasionally with shallow lobes, coarsely toothed; upper surface bright green; lower surface paler, hairy when young, smooth later. Flowers white, about 1 inch across, in clusters of 2 to 5; petals 5, narrowing at the base; fragrant. Fruit yellowish-green, 1 to 1¼ inches across, globe-shaped, fleshy, bitter. Occurs in low, open or upland woods, thickets along streams and prairie openings.

Prairie crab apple *(Malus ioensis)*
A large, thorny shrub to small tree up to 20 feet tall, with low, crooked branches; thicket-forming from sucker roots. Leaves alternate, simple, 1½ to 5 inches long, ¾ to 4 inches wide, widest at or below the middle; margins with shallow lobes, toothed; upper surface dark green, shiny; lower surface pale with white, densely matted hairs. Flowers white or pink, about ½ inch across, in clusters of 2 to 5; petals 5, narrowing at the base; fragrant. Fruit greenish to yellow, sometimes dotted, ¾ to 1½ inches across, globe-shaped, fleshy, bitter. Occurs in prairies, open woods, thickets, borders of woods and pastures, and along streams.

Narrow-leaved crab apple

Sweet crab apple

Prairie crab apple

WILD PLUMS

Wild plum, American plum
(Prunus americana)
A shrub or small tree up to 20 feet tall, forming thickets from root sprouts, with spreading, somewhat hanging branches; twigs sometimes thorny. Leaves alternate, simple, 2½ to 4 inches long, 1½ to 2 inches wide, broadest at or below the middle; margins sharply toothed; upper surface dark green; lower surface paler and net-veined. Flowers white, ¾ to 1¼ inch across in clusters of 2 to 6; petals 5, base narrow; fragrant. Fruit red or sometimes yellow, with pale dots, in clusters, globe-shaped, ¾ to 1 inch long, edible. Occurs in woodlands, pastures and thickets.

Wild goose plum *(Prunus munsoniana)*
A large shrub or small tree up to 25 feet tall, with an irregular, open crown. Leaves alternate, simple, 2½ to 4 inches long, ¾ to 1¼ inches wide, width fairly even throughout, somewhat folded lengthwise; margins finely toothed to rounded, with a gland on the inward-curved face; upper surface bright green, shiny; lower surface paler, slightly hairy. Flowers white, each ½ to ¾ inch across, in clusters; petals 5, narrow at the base; fragrant. Fruit red or yellow, white-dotted, with a thin, whitish coating, globe-shaped, about ¾ inch long, edible. Occurs in thickets, prairies, borders of streams and woodlands, and idle ground.

Chickasaw plum *(Prunus angustifolia)*
A twiggy shrub forming dense thickets, or a short-trunked, irregularly branched small tree up to 25 feet tall, the twigs often with thornlike spurs. Leaves alternate, simple, ¾ to 2 inches long, ¼ to ¾ inch wide, width even throughout and folded, with the tip curled down; margins bearing a gland between teeth; upper surface bright yellowish-green, shiny; lower surface paler, smooth. Flowers white, about ¼ inch across, in clusters; petals 5, narrow at the base; fragrant. Fruit red or yellow with yellow dots, globe-shaped, ½ to ¾ inch across, in clusters; edible. Occurs in thickets, pastures and fields, and along fencerows, roadsides and prairie streams.

ALTERNATE, SIMPLE

WILD PLUMS CONT'D, CHOKE CHERRY

Hortulan plum, wild goose plum
(Prunus hortulana)
A many-stemmed shrub or small tree up to 30 feet tall, with a broad, round-topped crown; twigs occasionally with thorns. Leaves alternate, simple, 4 to 6 inches long, 1 to 1½ inches wide, broadest at or below the middle; margins finely toothed, with a gland at the tip of each spreading tooth; upper surface dark green, shiny; lower surface paler, smooth or slightly hairy. Flowers white, ¾ to 1 inch across, in clusters; petals 5, narrow at the base. Fruit shiny red or yellow-red, with white dots, globe-shaped, ¾ to 1 inch across, edible. Occurs in open woodlands, borders of woods and thickets, and along streams.

Big tree plum *(Prunus mexicana)*
A large shrub or small tree up to 25 feet tall, with an irregular, open crown. Leaves alternate, simple, 1¾ to 3½ inches long, 1 to 2 inches wide, broadest at or below the middle; margins toothed; upper surface yellowish-green; lower surface paler, hairy. Flowers white, about ¾ to 1 inch across, in clusters of 2 to 4; petals 5, narrow at the base. Fruit grayish-blue or grayish-lavender with a whitish coating, globe-shaped, 1¼ to 1½ inches across, edible. Occurs in rocky or open woodlands and thickets.

Choke cherry *(Prunus virginiana)*
A large shrub or small tree up to 30 feet tall, with erect to horizontal branches, sometimes forming thickets from root sprouts. Leaves alternate, simple, ¾ to 4 inches long, ½ to 2 inches wide, broadest in the middle to uniformly wide, tip abrupt and sharp-pointed; margins sharply toothed; upper surface dark green, shiny; lower surface paler, somewhat hairy on the veins; leaf stalk with small glands near the leaf base. Flowers white; about ¼ to ½ inch across, many-flowered in dense, elongated clusters; petals 5. Fruit in elongated clusters; cherries dark red or nearly black, shiny, fleshy, round, ¼ to ⅜ inch across, bitter. Occurs on moist, mostly north-facing wooded slopes, bluffs and ravines.

PEACH, PERFUMED CHERRY, BLACK CHOKEBERRY

Peach *(Prunus persica)*
A large shrub to small tree up to 24 feet tall, with a rounded crown and spreading branches. Leaves alternate, simple, 3 to 6 inches long, ¾ to 2 inches wide; width fairly even throughout, somewhat folded lengthwise; margins finely toothed; both surfaces green, smooth, shiny. Flowers pink to rose-colored, 1 to 2 inches across, single or 2 together; petals 5; fragrant. Fruit globe-shaped, 2 to 3¼ inches across, velvety to densely hairy with matted wool, fleshy, edible. Native to China; commonly planted and escapes from cultivation to thickets, fencerows and roadsides.

Perfumed cherry *(Prunus mahaleb)*
A large shrub to small tree up to 26 feet tall, with low branches, often forming small thickets around the parent plant. Leaves alternate, simple, 1 to 3 inches long, ¾ to 1 inch wide, broadest at or below the middle; margins with rounded teeth; upper surface dark green, shiny; lower surface paler, with a few hairs along the central vein. Flowers white, about ¾ inch across, in clusters; petals 5. Fruit dark reddish-purple, somewhat elongated, about ⅜ inch long, ¼ inch across, bitter. Native of Europe; escapes from cultivation and forms thickets along roadsides and fencerows and into wooded areas.

Black chokeberry *(Aronia melanocarpa)*
A small shrub up to 9 feet tall, mostly single-stemmed; thickets are not dense, and sucker sprouts from roots are not apparent. Leaves alternate, simple, 1½ to 4 inches long, ¾ to 2 inches wide, longer than broad and tapering at both ends, sometimes broadest at the middle; margins finely toothed, with a small gland at the end of each tooth; upper surface dark green with reddish dots (glands) along the main vein, veins slightly sunken below the surface; lower surface paler, smooth, with a few scattered hairs. Flowers white to pinkish, 1 to 2 inches across, in clusters of 6 to 8 at the ends of twigs; petals 5, narrow at the base. Fruit purplish-black, about ¼ inch long and wide, tip rounded, base flattened. Occurs only in sandy, wet or boggy ground along seeps at the base of Crowley's Ridge. Endangered in Missouri.

Peach

Perfumed cherry

Black chokeberry

ALTERNATE, SIMPLE

WILLOWS

Carolina willow, Ward's willow
(Salix caroliniana)
A shrub to small tree up to 30 feet tall, with branches spreading or drooping to form an open, irregular crown. Leaves alternate, simple, 2 to 7 inches long, ⅜ to ¾ inch wide, narrowly lance-shaped; margins finely toothed; upper surface bright green; lower surface white to silvery-white; stipules (leafy appendages) at base of leaf stalk about ¾ inch across. Flowers in male and female catkins on separate plants. Fruit a capsule, clustered in catkins about 3 inches long. Occurs along gravel bars, sandy gravel beds and rocky banks of streams.

Missouri willow *(Salix eriocephala)*
A shrub to small- or medium-sized tree up to 50 feet tall, with slender branches that form a narrow crown. Leaves alternate, simple, 1½ to 3 inches long, ¼ to ¾ inch wide, lance-shaped to slightly broadest in the middle; margins finely toothed, tightly spaced; upper surface dark green to yellowish-green; lower surface pale, lightly coated with a white, waxy coating; stipules (leafy appendages) about ½ inch wide at base of leaf stalk. Flowers in male and female catkins on separate plants. Fruit a capsule, clustered in catkins 2 to 3 inches long. Occurs in floodplains along large rivers and their tributaries.

Sandbar willow *(Salix exigua)*
A slender, upright shrub forming thickets by spreading roots, or a small tree to 30 feet tall. Leaves alternate, simple, 2 to 6 inches long, ⅛ to ⅜ inch wide, width uniform throughout; margins with scattered, gland-tipped, unevenly spaced teeth; upper surface dark green; lower surface paler, hairy. Flowers in male and female catkins on separate plants. Fruit a capsule, clustered in catkins 1½ to 2 inches long. Occurs on sandbars, mudflats and alluvial muddy banks of streams, oxbow lakes, ponds and ditches. Formerly known as *Salix interior*.

Carolina willow, Ward's willow

Missouri willow

Sandbar willow

WILLOWS CONT'D

Meadow willow *(Salix petiolaris)*
A low-growing shrub to a height of 8 feet. Leaves alternate, simple, 1¼ to 3 inches long, about ½ inch wide, lance-shaped; margins finely toothed and tipped with glands, lower part of leaf lacking teeth; upper surface dark green, somewhat glossy, smooth; lower surface paler, smooth. Flowers in male and female catkins on separate plants. Fruit a capsule, clustered in catkins ¾ to 1 inch long. Occurs in low wet ground in mud or sandy gravel along streams. Also known as *Salix gracilis* var. *textoris*. Endangered in Missouri.

Silky willow *(Salix sericea)*
A shrub to small tree up to 15 feet tall, with clustered stems that are brittle and easy to break. Leaves alternate, simple, 2 to 3 inches long, ½ to ¾ inch wide, narrowly lance-shaped; margins finely toothed; upper surface dark green, hairy to smooth; lower surface with dense, silvery, silky hairs. Flowers in male and female catkins on separate plants. Fruit a capsule, clustered in catkins about 1¼ inches long. Occurs in fens and in swampy ground around springs and spring branches in the eastern part of the Ozarks.

Prairie willow *(Salix humilis)*
A shrub from 3 to 9 feet tall with wandlike branches. Leaves alternate, simple, 1¼ to 4 inches long, ¼ to ¾ inch wide, blade lance-shaped to narrowly broadest above the middle; margins smooth or wavy with rounded teeth; upper surface grayish-green, slightly hairy; lower surface silvery white with hairs; leafy appendages at base of leaf stalk lance-shaped, very short, dropping early. Flowers in male and female catkins on separate plants. Fruit a capsule, clustered in catkins ¾ to 1¼ inches long. Occurs in prairies, hill prairies, open woods, rocky draws or washes, rocky slopes, thickets, roadsides and railroad prairies.

ALTERNATE, SIMPLE

WILLOWS CONT'D, MEADOWSWEET, HARDHACK

Pussy willow *(Salix discolor)*
A large shrub to small tree up to 16 feet tall, with the trunks single or clustered. Leaves alternate, simple, 1½ to 3¼ inches long, ¾ to 1¼ inches wide, width even throughout, the tip slightly pointed down; margins irregularly toothed and wavy; upper surface dark green, semishiny; lower surface with a whitish coating. Flowers with male and female catkins on separate plants. Fruit a capsule, clustered in catkins about 3 inches long, catkins wide and spreading, showy. Occurs along creeks and rivers in open or wooded areas. Endangered in Missouri. The pussy willow sold in florist shops is goat willow (*Salix caprea*), a native of Europe and Asia.

Meadowsweet *(Spiraea alba* var. *alba)*
A shrub to 4 feet tall, finely branched; often forming small colonies. Leaves alternate, simple, 1¼ to 2 inches long, about ½ inch wide, narrowly broadest below the middle to lance-shaped; margins with fine hairs, sharply toothed except on the lower portion; both surfaces green, smooth or slightly hairy. Flowers white, ⅛ inch across, numerous, in conical to pyramidal clusters, 3 to 4 inches long, 1½ to 2½ inches wide; petals 5, with ends cupped and wavy margins. Fruit podlike with 5 parts, each splitting to release 3 to 10 seeds. Occurs in wet river bottom prairies, wet prairies along railroads, alluvial soils bordering oxbow lakes of rivers and open ground along streams. Endangered in Missouri.

Hardhack, steeple bush *(Spiraea tomentosa)*
A shrub, simple or sparingly branched, attaining a height of 4 feet. Leaves alternate, simple, 1¼ to 2½ inches long, ⅜ to 1¼ inches wide, broadest in the middle; margins unequally toothed, lacking teeth
near the base, leathery; upper surface dark green and hairy; lower surface white or rusty with densely hairy, matted wool. Flowers pink, sometimes white, ⅛ to ¼ inch across, numerous, in spirelike clusters 2 to 8 inches long, stalks densely hairy with matted wool. Fruit podlike with 5 parts, each splitting to release 4 to 7 seeds. Occurs in low, seepy areas; known in Missouri from only one site. The Dunklin County site is an old record. Endangered in Missouri.

Pussy willow

Meadowsweet

Hardhack, steeple bush

ALTERNATE, SIMPLE

WILD BLUEBERRIES

Highbush blueberry, farkleberry
(Vaccinium arboreum)
A stiff-branched shrub or small, crooked tree up to 20 feet tall. Leaves alternate, simple, sometimes evergreen, leathery, 1 to 3 inches long, about 1 inch wide, oval to broadest above the middle; margins entire or slightly toothed; upper surface dark green, shiny; lower surface dull green, slightly hairy. Flowers white or pinkish, in loose, drooping clusters in the axils of leaves, about ⅜ inch long, bell-shaped, with 5-lobed petals curled at the tip; stamens not extending beyond the petals. Fruit black, shiny, sweet, about ⅜ inch wide, globe-shaped. Occurs in acid soils overlying sandstone, chert or igneous bedrock in rocky, open woods; on dry slopes and ridges; and along bluffs and glades.

Deerberry, highbush huckleberry
(Vaccinium stamineum)
A shrub, irregularly branched, rarely more than 6 feet tall. Leaves alternate, simple, ¾ to 2¾ inches long, ½ to 1 inch wide, slightly broader above the middle; margins lacking teeth, fringed with hairs; upper surface dull, light to yellow-green, mostly smooth; lower surface duller and hairy; smaller leaves (bracts) present at the base of flower and fruit stalks. Flowers white to pinkish, about ¼ inch across, bell-shaped, hanging in clusters of 3 to 10; petals with 5 lobes; stamens extending beyond the petals. Fruit reddish- to dark purple, about ¼ inch in diameter, globe-shaped, somewhat sweet. Occurs in acid soils over sandstone, chert and igneous bedrock; in rocky, open, dry woods; and on ridges, upland slopes and glades.

Lowbush blueberry *(Vaccinium pallidum)*
A low, stiff-branched shrub ½ to 3 feet high, often in extensive colonies. Leaves alternate, simple, ¾ to 1¾ inches long, ½ to 1 inch wide, oval to broadest above the middle; margins entire or finely toothed; upper surface pale green, glossy, smooth; lower surface pale green, hairy or smooth. Flowers white, pink or red, about ¼ inch long, longer than broad, in clusters; petals a short tube with 5 lobes; stamens not extending beyond the petals. Fruit dull dark blue to almost black, about ¼ inch across, globe-shaped, sweet. Occurs in dry, rocky, open woods, and in acid soils overlying sandstone, chert or igneous bedrock. Previously known as *Vaccinium vacillans*.

Highbush blueberry, farkleberry

Deerberry, highbush huckleberry

Lowbush blueberry

BLACK HUCKLEBERRY, HOLLIES

Black huckleberry *(Gaylussacia baccata)*

A rigid, upright, much-branched shrub attaining a height of 1 to 4 feet. Leaves alternate, simple, ¾ to 1¾ inches long, ½ to ¾ inch wide, oval or broadest below the middle; margins lacking teeth; upper surface yellowish-green, smooth; lower surface paler, hairy or smooth, with minute sticky, resinous dots. Flowers pink or reddish, hanging down, ¼ inch long, conical to round; petals a short tube with 5 lobes curved outward; stamens not extending beyond the petals. Fruit black, about ¼ inch long, shiny, sweet. Occurs on rocky, wooded ridges above bluffs, usually in cherty soils. Known in Missouri from two sites. Endangered in Missouri.

Possum haw, deciduous holly *(Ilex decidua)*

Usually a shrub with a spreading, open crown, but sometimes a small tree to 30 feet tall, with spurred (shortened) lateral twigs. Leaves alternate, simple, 2 to 3 inches long, ½ to 1½ inches wide, widest at the middle and tapering at both ends, tip blunt; margins mostly with round or blunt teeth; upper surface dark green; lower surface paler, smooth or hairy on the veins. Flowers white; male and female flowers mostly on separate plants in small clusters; petals 4 to 6, about ¼ inch across. Fruit red, rarely orange, ¼ inch across, globe-shaped. Occurs on dolomite glades; in rocky, upland, open woods; in low wet woods along streams and lowlands; in borders of woods; and along fencerows.

Winterberry *(Ilex verticillata)*

A shrub or small, rounded tree up to 25 feet tall. Leaves alternate, simple, 1½ to 4 inches long, about 1 inch wide, broadest at or below the middle, tip tapering to a point; margins with sharp-pointed teeth; upper surface dark green; lower surface paler, downy. Flowers white; male and female flowers mostly on separate plants in small clusters; petals 4, about ¼ inch across. Fruit shiny red to orange or yellow, about ¼ inch across, globe-shaped. Occurs along igneous shut-ins, rocky streambeds and sandstone bluffs of the St. Francois Mountains. Rare in Missouri.

WATER ELM, BUCKTHORNS

Water elm *(Planera aquatica)*
A large shrub or small tree up to 40 feet tall, growing in swampy ground. Base of trunk frequently inundated during wet seasons. Leaves alternate, simple, 2 to 4 inches long, ½ to 1 inch wide, broadest at the middle, base uneven; margins toothed; upper surface dark green; lower surface paler. Flowers greenish-yellow; male and female flowers on the same plant, in clusters of 2 to 5; petals absent. Fruit about ⅜ inch long, broadest below the middle, covered with an irregular warty surface, leathery. Occurs in swamps and low wet bottomland forests.

Carolina buckthorn *(Rhamnus caroliniana)*
A shrub or small tree up to 35 feet tall, with a trunk diameter of up to 8 inches. Leaves alternate, simple, 2 to 6 inches long, 1 to 2 inches wide, broadest at the middle to uniformly wide; margins slightly toothed; upper surface bright green, smooth, shiny; lower surface velvety-hairy to slightly hairy to smooth. Flowers greenish-yellow, hairy, about ¼ inch across, single or in clusters of 2 to 10 arising from leaf axils; petals 5. Fruit red at first, turning black and shiny, about ¼ inch across, round, sweet. Occurs in low woodlands in valleys along streams, and in rocky, wooded slopes, upland ridges, thickets and glades.

Lance-leaved buckthorn *(Rhamnus lanceolata)*
A small to large shrub up to 9 feet tall, with an erect and widely branched habit. Leaves alternate, simple, 1 to 3¼ inches long, ½ to 1 inch wide, lance-shaped to uniformly wide along its length; margins finely toothed with teeth curving inward; upper surface dull green, smooth; lower surface paler, somewhat hairy. Flowers greenish-yellow, about ⅛ inch across, single or in clusters arising from leaf axils, with male and female flowers on the same plant; petals 4. Fruit black, about ¼ inch across, globe-shaped with a thin white coating. Occurs on open wooded slopes, in thickets and on glades; usually on rocky limestone or dolomite surfaces.

ALTERNATE, SIMPLE

Water elm

Carolina buckthorn

Lance-leaved buckthorn

BUCKTHORNS, LEATHERWOOD

Woolly buckthorn, gum bumelia, chittim wood *(Bumelia lanuginosa)*

A shrub or an irregularly shaped tree up to 40 feet tall, with thorns, short spur branches, and milky sap. Leaves alternate or clustered, simple, leathery, 1 to 3 inches long, about 1 inch wide, widest near the tip; margins lacking teeth; upper surface shiny green, smooth; lower surface varying from rusty to white or gray-woolly. Flowers white, about ⅛ inch long, in dense clusters where the leaf joins the stem; petals 5, fused to form a tube. Fruit shiny, black, oval, about ½ inch across, on slender drooping stalks, bittersweet, edible. Occurs in dry or rocky open woodlands, glades and bluff escarpments; usually on upland ridges and slopes; rarely in valleys and ravine bottoms. Also known as *Sideroxylon lanuginosum*.

Southern buckthorn *(Bumelia lycioides)*

A large shrub or small tree up to 25 feet tall, with spreading branches, stout thorns, short spur branches, and milky sap. Leaves alternate, simple, 2 to 6 inches long, ½ to 2 inches wide, broadest at or above the middle; margins lacking teeth; upper surface bright green; lower surface paler, lacking hairs. Flowers white, about ⅛ inch long, in dense clusters where the leaf joins the stem; petals 5, fused to form a tube. Fruit black, about ½ inch long, oval to broadest below the middle, abruptly pointed at the tip, on slender drooping stalks, bittersweet, edible. Occurs in low wet woods of floodplains and river bottoms, and in thickets along streams. Also known as *Sideroxylon lycioides*.

Leatherwood *(Dirca palustris)*

A widely branching shrub up to 7 feet tall, with a single trunk. Twigs very flexible and capable of being tied into knots without breaking; enlarged at the joints. Leaves alternate, simple, 2 to 4 inches long, about 2¾ inches wide, oval to broadest above the middle; margins lacking teeth; upper surface light green, smooth; lower surface with a whitish coat and somewhat hairy. Flowers yellow, about ⅜ inch long, in clusters of 2 to 4 flowers arising before the leaves appear; petals absent; stamens 8. Fruit red to orange, ¼ to ⅜ inch long, oval. Occurs in low bottom woods on terraces above streams or on rich and wooded lower slopes.

Woolly buckthorn, gum bumelia, chittim wood

Southern buckthorn

Leatherwood

HAWTHORNS, SNOW WREATH

Frosty hawthorn *(Crataegus pruinosa)*
A thorny shrub or small tree attaining a height of 20 feet and a trunk diameter of 4 to 8 inches. Twigs with stout thorns, ½ to 1½ inches long. Leaves alternate, simple, firm, leathery, 1 to 1½ inches long, ¾ to 1 inch wide, broadest in the middle; margins densely toothed and also short-lobed; upper surface dark green, smooth; lower surface paler, smooth. Flowers white, ¾ to 1 inch across, showy, in clusters of 6 or less; petals 5. Fruit green or red, about ½ inch across, globe-shaped, smooth, shiny, with a white waxy coating, often dotted. Occurs in rocky open woods and thickets.

One-flowered hawthorn *(Crataegus uniflora)*
A slender shrub 3 to 12 feet tall, rarely a small tree, with crooked, small branches. Base of twigs bearing one thorn, ½ to 2¼ inches long. Leaves alternate, simple, ¾ to 1¼ inches long, ½ to 1 inch wide or larger, broadest at or above the middle; margins toothed; upper surface dark green, shiny; lower surface paler, hairy. Flowers white, single, ⅜ to ⅝ inch wide; flower stalk densely hairy with matted wool; petals 5. Fruit greenish-yellow to dull red, ⅜ to ½ inch across, globe-shaped, hairy. Occurs in thickets and open woods, usually in sandy or rocky ground.

Snow wreath *(Neviusia alabamensis)*
A small shrub 3 to 6 feet tall, characterized by arching branches, short lateral branches and the stem sprouting by way of root suckers. Leaves alternate, simple, ¾ to 2½ inches long, ½ to 1 ¾ inches wide, broadest at or below the middle; margins sharply and densely toothed; upper surface light green, slightly hairy; lower surface with gland-tipped hairs. Flowers white, opening with expanding leaves, in clusters of 1 to 4 flowers, with a green, leafy, 5-parted calyx instead of petals, about 1 inch across; stamens white, usually more than 100. Fruit a dry capsule with a single seed. Occurs along wooded slopes below bluffs or ridges on talus or rocky soils; also sandy loam. Last reported in Missouri in 1918, 8 miles west of Poplar Bluff.

Frosty hawthorn

One-flowered hawthorn

Snow wreath

ALDER, BARBERRIES

Alder *(Alnus serrulata)*
An irregularly shaped shrub or slender small tree up to 20 feet tall. Leaves alternate, simple, 1 to 5 inches long, 1½ to 2½ inches wide, broadest at or above the middle; margins with blunt or rounded teeth; upper surface dark green; lower surface dark green, somewhat hairy. Flowers with male and female catkins on the same twig; male catkins 2 to 4 inches long; female catkins about ¼ inch long; petals absent. Fruit about ¾ inch long, oval, conical, with a cluster of woody bracts, each below a small seed (nutlet), each less than ⅛ inch long. Occurs along stream banks, springs, spring branches and fens.

American barberry *(Berberis canadensis)*
A small, spiny shrub, sparsely branched, less than 3 feet tall. Leaves alternate or whorled, simple, ¾ to 2½ inches long, ⅜ to 1 inch wide, broadest above the middle and narrowly tapering to the base; margins with several small teeth, 2 to 11 on each side; upper surface dark green, smooth; lower surface paler, smooth. Spines at the leaf axils are actually three-branched, modified leaves that bear clusters of small leaves at their base. Flowers yellow, about ¼ inch long, in clusters of 5 to 10 flowers; petals 6. Fruit red, about ⅜ inch long. Occurs on rocky, wooded (usually north-facing) upper ledges of bluffs along the Jacks Fork and Eleven Point rivers on dolomite or sandstone. Endangered in Missouri.

Japanese barberry *(Berberis thunbergii)*

Escapes from cultivation

A densely branched, spiny shrub up to 7 feet tall. Leaves alternate or whorled, simple, up to 2 inches long; up to ¾ inch wide, broadest at or above the middle, narrowly tapering to the base; margins lacking teeth; upper surface bright green, smooth; lower surface paler, with a white coating. A prominent single spine appears with a leaf cluster at each axil. Flowers yellow, about ⅜ inch across, in clusters of 2 to 4 flowers; petals 6. Fruit red, about ⅜ inch long. A native of Japan, commonly cultivated as a hedge plant, sometimes escaping into old fields and open woods. Another exotic shrub, common barberry (*Berberis vulgaris*), has clusters of 10 to 20 flowers, 13 to 20 teeth on each side of the leaf margins, with each tooth ending in a bristle.

MUSCLEWOOD, HOP HORNBEAM, HAZELNUT

Musclewood, American hornbeam
(Carpinus caroliniana)
A tall shrub or small tree up to 35 feet tall, with a smooth gray trunk and hanging branches. Trunk fluted into musclelike ridges. Leaves alternate, simple, 2 to 5 inches long, 1 to 2 inches wide, broadest at the middle; margins densely toothed; upper surface dull bluish-green, smooth; lower surface paler, hairy in the vein axils. Flowers in male and female catkins on the same twig; male catkins 1 to 1½ inches long; female catkins about ½ inch long; petals lacking. Fruit in long, hanging clusters of paired 3-lobed bracts (modified leaves), with each pair of bracts having at its base a small seed (nutlet). Occurs on north-facing bluffs, in rich woods at the bases of bluffs, on rocky slopes along streams, and in ravine bottoms, low wooded valleys and moist woodlands.

Hop hornbeam, ironwood *(Ostrya virginiana)*
A small tree up to 24 feet tall, with wide, spreading branches. Leaves alternate, simple, 2½ to 4½ inches long, 1½ to 2½ inches wide, broadly lance-shaped, base often uneven; margins sharply and densely toothed; upper surface yellowish to dark green, dull; lower surface paler, hairy. Flowers appear before the leaves in male and female catkins on the same twig; male catkins 1½ to 3 inches long; female catkins about ¼ inch long. Fruit in conelike clusters resembling hops, 1½ to 2 inches long; each scale-like sac contains a single nut about ¼ inch long. Occurs in fairly dry soils on rocky slopes, along bluffs, in upland woods and rarely along streams.

Hazelnut *(Corylus americana)*
A thicket-forming, spreading shrub attaining a height of 3 to 10 feet. Leaves alternate, simple, 3 to 6 inches long, 2 to 4½ inches wide, broadest below the middle to oval; margins finely and densely toothed; upper surface dark green, somewhat rough; lower surface paler, with matted hairs or more or less hairy. Flowers appear before the leaves in male and female catkins on the same twig; male catkins 3 to 4 inches long; female catkins much shorter; petals lacking. Fruit ½ to 1½ inches long, encased in large bracts (modified leaves) in clusters of 2 to 6; nut light brown, about ½ inch long, sweet, edible. Occurs in dry or moist thickets, woodlands and borders of woodlands; in valleys and uplands; and in prairies.

Musclewood, American hornbeam

Hop hornbeam, ironwood

Hazelnut

GOOSEBERRIES, AMERICAN BLACK CURRANT

Missouri gooseberry, wild gooseberry
(Ribes missouriense)
A thorny shrub up to 3 feet tall, spreading to 6 feet wide, with clustered trunks and arching branches; the many spines ¼ to ¾ inch long, solitary or in pairs or trios. Leaves alternate, simple, ¾ to 2½ inches long or wide; outline rounded, cut into 3 to 5 lobes that, in turn, are coarsely toothed or bluntly lobed; upper surface green, smooth; lower surface soft-hairy or smooth later. Flowers whitish-green, ¼ to ¾ inch long, single or in clusters of 2 to 4; petals 5; stamens much extended. Fruit blackish-purple, smooth, globe-shaped, about ¼ inch across, edible. Occurs in rocky or open dry woods, thickets, upland or lowland woodland borders and grazed or cutover areas.

Prickly gooseberry *(Ribes cynosbati)*
A low, straggly shrub with rigid, spreading or trailing branches. Generally armed with slender spines along the stem to ¾ inch long. Leaves alternate, simple, 1 to 2 inches long and wide, round to broadly egg-shaped; margins 3- to 5-lobed, lobes with teeth rounded to pointed; both surfaces hairy, undersurface more so. Flowers yellowish-green, about ½ inch long, single or in clusters of 2 to 4 flowers, base of flower bristly; petals 5; stamens barely showing beyond the petals. Fruit reddish-purple, globe-shaped, ¼ to ½ inch in diameter, armed with stiff prickles. Occurs on north-facing, shaded bluffs and wooded ledges; often seen dangling its stems over the faces of rocks.

American black currant *(Ribes americanum)*
An erect or spreading, spineless shrub attaining a height of 5 feet. Leaves alternate, simple, 1 to 3 inches long or wide; outline circular, lobes 3 to 5, sharply pointed to blunt; margins irregularly toothed; upper surface dull green, smooth; lower surface somewhat hairy and dotted with numerous minute, orange glands. Flowers greenish-white or yellowish, ⅜ to ½ inch long, in drooping clusters 1 to 3 inches long, with 2 to 12 flowers; petals 5; stamens not extending beyond the flower. Fruit black, smooth, globe-shaped, ¼ to ½ inch across, in drooping clusters 1½ to 3 inches long, edible. Occurs on moist wooded hillsides and margins of fens. Endangered in Missouri.

GOLDEN CURRANT, SPICE BUSH, PONDBERRY

Golden currant *(Ribes odoratum)*
An erect, spineless shrub attaining a height of 6 feet. Leaves alternate, simple, 1⅜ to 3¼ inches long or wide, circular, with 3 to 5 lobes either entire or toothed toward the tip; margins often fringed with hairs; both surfaces green and hairy on the veins. Flowers golden yellow, fragrant, about ½ inch long, cylindrical, in clusters of 4 to 10, nodding; petals 5. Fruit black, about ¼ inch across, smooth, globe-shaped, edible. Occurs on exposed, high, rocky limestone or dolomite bluffs, often on narrow ledges.

Spice bush *(Lindera benzoin)*
A stout shrub of damp woods attaining a height of 14 feet, usually with several stems from the base. All parts of the shrub are aromatic. Leaves alternate, simple, nondrooping, aromatic when crushed, 2 to 6 inches long, 1 to 3 inches wide, broadest at or above the middle, tip abruptly pointed, base narrowing at a sharp angle; margins lacking teeth; upper surface bright green; lower surface whitish. Flowers appearing before the leaves, yellow, fragrant, about ¼ inch across, in clusters of 3 to 6 along the stem, with male and female flowers on separate plants; petals absent; sepals 6; stamens 9. Fruit glossy red, about ⅜ inch long, solitary or in clusters. Occurs in low or moist woodlands and thickets along streams; in valleys, ravine bottoms and bases of bluffs; and along spring branches and seepage of wooded slopes.

Pondberry *(Lindera melissifolia)*
A strong-scented colonial shrub, 2 to 6 feet tall, growing in low wet woods. Leaves alternate, simple, drooping, aromatic when crushed, 2 to 6 inches long, ¾ to 2¼ inches wide, tapering at each end and broadest in the middle, tip abruptly pointed, base narrowing at a sharp angle; margins lacking teeth; both surfaces dark green, somewhat hairy, becoming smooth later. Flowers appearing before the leaves, yellow, fragrant, about ¼ inch across, in clusters of 3 to 6 along the stem, with male and female flowers on separate plants; petals absent; sepals 6; stamens 9. Fruit glossy red, about ⅜ inch long, solitary or in clusters. Occurs in low wet, sandy woods in Ripley County. Endangered in Missouri.

WITCH-HAZELS, WILD AZALEA

Ozark witch-hazel *(Hamamelis vernalis)*
A shrub attaining a height of up to 9 feet, often sending up sprouts from the base; or uncommonly a small tree, especially in cultivation; twigs densely velvety-hairy. Leaves alternate, simple, 2 to 5 inches long, about 3 inches wide, broadest above the middle, base unequal; margins strongly wavy; upper surface dull green with veins indented; lower surface paler, smooth to hairy, veins prominent. Flowers yellow to dark red, from January to March, ¼ to ½ inch long, in clusters; petals 4, narrow, strap- or ribbon-shaped; fragrant. Fruit a woody capsule, about ½ inch long, splitting to propel seeds up to 30 feet. Occurs in gravel and rocky streambeds.

Eastern witch-hazel *(Hamamelis virginiana)*
A tall shrub or small tree up to 30 feet tall, with a short trunk, soon branching to form a broad, rounded shape; twigs smooth or slightly hairy. Leaves alternate, simple, 3 to 6 inches long, about 3 inches wide, broadest above the middle, base uneven; margins strongly wavy, sometimes toothed; upper surface dull green; lower surface somewhat hairy. Flowers bright yellow, from October to December, ½ to ¾ inch long, in clusters; petals 4, narrow, strap- or ribbon-shaped; fragrant. Fruit a woody capsule, about ½ inch long, splitting to propel seeds up to 30 feet. Occurs in moist woods on north- or east-facing slopes or in wooded valleys along streams.

Wild azalea *(Rhododendron prinophyllum)*
An erect shrub to 9 feet tall, with picturesque ascending branches, often sending up new stems from roots. Leaves alternate, simple, usually clustered at or near the tip of twigs, 1½ to 3½ inches long, ¾ to 1½ inches wide, broadest at or above the middle; margins lacking teeth, fringed with hairs; upper surface green, finely hairy; lower surface densely hairy. Flowers pink, very fragrant, 1½ to 2 inches across, tubular, dense with gland-tipped hairs, in clusters of 6 to 8; petals 5, spreading; stamens 5, extending much beyond the flower. Fruit a capsule, cylindrical, densely hairy, about ½ inch long. Occurs in acid soils overlying sandstone, chert or igneous rock; on north-facing, steep wooded slopes of ravines; small bluffs; slopes along streams; upland ridges; and shallow draws. Formerly known as *Rhododendron roseum*.

Ozark witch-hazel

Eastern witch-hazel

Wild azalea

SNOWBELL, CORKWOOD, VIRGINIA WILLOW

Snowbell *(Styrax americanum)*
A widely branched shrub attaining a height of 3 to 9 feet. Leaves alternate, simple, ¾ to 4 inches long, ½ to 1½ inches wide, broadest at the middle and tapering at both ends; margins entire to mostly toothed; upper surface dark green, smooth; lower surface paler, slightly hairy to smooth. Flowers white, fragrant, about ¼ inch long, drooping, in clusters of 2 to 4; petals 5, narrow, slightly hairy to smooth. Fruit globe-shaped, about ¼ inch across, with fine, dense hairs, splitting into three parts to release the seeds. Occurs in bald cypress and tupelo swamps and low wet woods.

Corkwood *(Leitneria floridana)*
A shrub or small tree up to 20 feet tall, often forming thickets from root suckers. Leaves alternate, simple, at the ends of twigs, 3 to 6 inches long, 1 to 3 inches wide, broadest in the middle; margins lacking teeth; upper surface dark olive to dull green; lower surface paler, with long, soft hairs. Flowers in catkins, with male and female flowers on separate plants; catkins flowering before leaves emerge. Fruit flattened, brown, ¾ inch long, ¼ to ⅜ inch wide, in clusters of 2 to 6. Occurs in wooded or open wetlands and in wet ditches along roadsides. Endangered in Missouri.

Virginia willow, sweet-spire *(Itea virginica)*
A slender-branched shrub up to 10 feet tall, sometimes almost reclining. Leaves alternate, simple, 1 to 3 inches long, ½ to 1⅜ inches wide, rather thin, widest at or below the middle; margins sharply toothed; upper surface dull green, smooth; lower surface hairy to smooth. Flowers white or pink, about ⅛ inch long, numerous in drooping clusters 2 to 5 inches long; petals 5. Fruit a capsule, ¼ inch long, narrow, with a pointed tip. Occurs in swamps, in low wet woods and along sandy spring branches.

NEW JERSEY TEA, REDROOT, BUCKBRUSH

New Jersey tea (*Ceanothus americanus*)
A shrub to 3 feet tall, with spreading branches; herbaceous above, woody toward the base. Leaves alternate, simple, 2 to 4 inches long, 1 to 2½ inches wide, broadest at or below the middle, tip somewhat pointed; margins toothed; upper surface green, hairy; lower surface gray, densely velvety-hairy. Flowers white, minute, fragrant, in branched clusters 2 to 5 inches long on a stalk 2 to 10 inches long, at the base of leaves towards the top of the stem; petals 5, each resembling a miniature ladle. Fruit black, ⅛ to ¼ inch long, round, three-parted. Occurs in upland or rocky prairies, glades, open woods and thickets.

Redroot (*Ceanothus herbaceus*)
An upright shrub attaining a height of 3 feet, with slender, upright, hairy branches. Leaves alternate, simple, 1½ to 2½ inches long, ½ to 1 inch wide, leaf overall very narrow, but broad in the middle, tip mostly blunt; margins somewhat toothed; upper surface dark green, smooth to hairy; lower surface paler, hairy. Flowers white, minute, in branched clusters 1 to 2 inches long on a short stalk about ⅜ inch long at the base of leaves along the stem; petals 5, each resembling a miniature ladle. Fruit dark brown, about ⅛ inch long, round, three-parted. Occurs in upland and rocky prairies, loess hill prairies, glades and open rocky woodlands. Formerly called *Ceanothus ovatus*.

Buckbrush, maiden bush
(*Andrachne phyllanthoides*)
An upright or straggling, branched shrub from 1 to 3 feet tall. Leaves alternate, simple, ⅜ to ⅞ inch long, ⅜ to ¾ inch wide, thin, oval to broadest above the middle; margins lacking teeth; both surfaces yellowish-green, smooth; leaves with clear to milky sap when broken. Flowers greenish-yellow, minute, about ¼ inch wide on long stalks arising where leaf joins stem, with both male and female flowers found on the same plant; petals 5 together alternating with 5 sepals. Occurs on rocky ledges of dolomite bluffs, on dolomite glades and along dry, gravelly washes of rocky streambeds.

ALTERNATE, SIMPLE

EASTERN REDBUD, SERVICE BERRY, ALTERNATE-LEAVED DOGWOOD

Eastern redbud *(Cercis canadensis)*
A shrub or small tree up to 40 feet tall, flowering before the leaves emerge. Leaves alternate, simple, 2 to 6 inches long, 1¼ to 6 inches wide, oval to heart-shaped, sometimes broader than long; margins lacking teeth; upper surface dark green; lower surface paler, with some hairs along the veins. Flowers rose-purple, about ⅜ inch long, in clusters of 2 to 8; petals 5, in the typical pea-flower configuration. Fruit a pod 3 to 4 inches long, about ½ inch wide, leathery, persistent on the branches. Occurs in open woodlands, borders of woods, thickets, dolomite glades, and along rocky streams and bluffs.

Service berry, shadbush *(Amelanchier arborea)*
A tall shrub or small tree, rarely up to 30 feet tall, with a narrow, rounded crown and smooth, light gray bark, flowering before the leaves emerge. Leaves alternate, simple, 2 to 5 inches long, 1 to 2 inches wide, broadest at the middle; margins sharply and finely toothed; upper surface medium green; lower surface paler, hairy. Flowers white, ½ to 1 inch long, in dense clusters 3 to 5 inches long; petals 5; fragrant. Fruit reddish-purple, ¼ to ½ inch across, globe-shaped, slightly sweet, edible. Occurs in rocky open woods and bluffs, usually on well-drained slopes.

Alternate-leaved dogwood, pagoda dogwood *(Cornus alternifolia)*
A shrub or small tree up to 18 feet tall, with branches often in tiered layers. Leaves alternate (a few opposite), simple, often crowded near the end of twigs, 2 to 5 inches long, ¾ to 2½ inches wide, broadest at the middle; margins lacking teeth; upper surface dark green; lower surface paler, hairy. Flowers white, about ⅛ inch long, in broad, flat-topped clusters, 1¼ to 2½ inches across; petals 4, small. Fruit bluish-black, round, about ⅜ inch across, borne on a red stalk. Occurs along wooded north-facing slopes and along wooded banks of streams.

Eastern redbud

Service berry, shadbush

Alternate-leaved dogwood, pagoda dogwood

ALTERNATE, SIMPLE

DWARF CHESTNUT OAK, DWARF HACKBERRY, AMERICAN SMOKE TREE

Dwarf chestnut oak *(Quercus prinoides)*

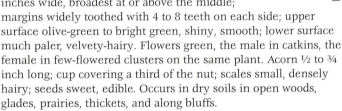

A shrub or small tree up to 15 feet tall, usually growing in clumps or thickets. Leaves alternate, simple, leathery, 1½ to 4 inches long, 1 to 2½ inches wide, broadest at or above the middle; margins widely toothed with 4 to 8 teeth on each side; upper surface olive-green to bright green, shiny, smooth; lower surface much paler, velvety-hairy. Flowers green, the male in catkins, the female in few-flowered clusters on the same plant. Acorn ½ to ¾ inch long; cup covering a third of the nut; scales small, densely hairy; seeds sweet, edible. Occurs in dry soils in open woods, glades, prairies, thickets, and along bluffs.

Dwarf hackberry *(Celtis tenuifolia)*

A shrub to small tree up to 24 feet tall, often somewhat straggly with some corky projections on the bark. Leaves alternate, simple, ¾ to 4 inches long, ½ to 1¾ inches wide, broadest near the base, base uneven, with 3 principal veins emerging; margins with few teeth; upper surface dark green, rough; lower surface paler, hairy to smooth. Flowers both male and female on the same plant in small clusters. Fruit orange to brown or red, about ¼ inch across, globe-shaped. Occurs in rocky open woods, dolomite glades and along bluffs.

American smoke tree *(Cotinus obovatus)*

A tall shrub to small tree up to 35 feet tall, with slender, spreading branches. Leaves alternate, simple, most abundant toward tip of twigs, bruised leaves somewhat fragrant, 1½ to 6 inches long, 2 to 3 inches wide, broadest in the middle; margins lacking teeth, wavy; upper surface bluish- or olive-green, smooth to hairy; lower surface hairy early and smooth with age. Flowers greenish yellow, ⅛ inch across, borne in loose, branching clusters, 5 to 6 inches long, at the end of stems, flower stalks feathery, purple or brown gland-tipped hairs; petals 5. Fruit kidney-shaped, flattened, about ¼ inch long; fruit stalks conspicuously purple or brown with gland-tipped hairs. Occurs on dolomite glades and wooded, rocky dolomite bluffs.

Dwarf chestnut oak

Dwarf hackberry

American smoke tree

JOINTWEED, NINEBARK, STAGGERBUSH

Jointweed *(Polygonella americana)*
A somewhat branched, stout shrub up to 4 feet tall, with foliage persisting through most of winter. Leaves alternate, simple, needlelike, often in clusters, fleshy, ¼ to 1½ inches long, narrow; margins lacking teeth; leaves gray-green. Flowers white or pink, about ¼ inch across, in clusters 1 to 3 inches long; petals 5, the inner 3 are rounded, the outer 2 are pointed. Fruit with 3 wings, hard, dry, rounded, about ⅛ inch long. Occurs in dry sandy soils, mainly on Crowley's Ridge in southeastern Missouri.

Ninebark *(Physocarpus opulifolius)*
A shrub 3 to 10 feet tall, with wide-spreading, graceful, recurved branches, and bark peeling off in conspicuous thin strips. Leaves alternate, simple, 2 to 4 inches long, 2 to 3½ inches wide, broadest below the middle to circular, often 3- to 5-lobed; margins with teeth pointed to rounded; upper surface dark green, smooth; lower surface paler, mostly smooth. Flowers white, about ¼ inch across, in dense clusters at the tips of twigs, 1 to 2½ inches broad; petals 5; stamens numerous (30–40). Fruit reddish, dried, ¼ to ½ inch long, in drooping clusters. Occurs on gravel bars, rocky banks, bluffs along streams, and in moist thickets.

Staggerbush *(Lyonia mariana)*
A shrub 3 to 6 feet tall, with erect, mostly smooth, black-dotted branches. Leaves alternate, simple, ¾ to 3 inches long, ⅜ to 1½ inches wide, broadest at or above the middle; margins lacking teeth; upper surface medium green, smooth; lower surface paler, slightly hairy, sometimes with black dots. Flowers white or pink, cylindrical, nodding, about ½ inch long, in clusters 1¼ to 4 inches long; petals 5 as small lobes. Fruit a capsule, pyramidal with a flattened base, about ¼ inch long. Occurs in sandy pine-oak woodlands. Known only from one site in one county in Missouri; not seen over the last 60 years.

AUTUMN OLIVE, MATRIMONY VINE, ROSE OF SHARON

Autumn olive *(Elaeagnus umbellata)*
A large, multistemmed shrub reaching 18 feet high and up to 25 feet across. Leaves alternate, simple, 1½ to 3 inches long, 1 to 1¼ inches wide, evenly wide throughout; margins lacking teeth, wavy; upper surface bright green; lower surface silvery green with silver scales, producing a shimmering appearance when windblown. Flowers cream to light yellow, fragrant, about 1 inch long, tubular, in clusters of 1 to 8 arising from leaf axils, outside of flowers with silver scales; petals 4, spreading. Fruit speckled red, about ¼ inch across, globe-shaped to broadest above the middle, bitter to semisweet. Native to Asia; planted along roadsides and fencerows; difficult to control; spreads into fields, pastures, edges of woods and edges of streams.

Matrimony vine *(Lycium barbarum)*
A shrub growing erect or with recurved and drooping branches, sometimes trailing or vinelike, attaining a length of 3 to 10 feet (rarely more than 3 to 5 feet when erect). Spines about ½ inch long when present. Leaves alternate, simple, ½ to 2¼ inches long, ¼ to 1 inch wide, oval to lance-shaped, base tapering to a leaf stalk; margins lacking teeth; upper and lower surfaces grayish-green, smooth. Flowers greenish to purplish, about ¼ inch long, in clusters of 2 to 4; petals as 5 lobes at end of short tube. Fruit a berry, orange-red or scarlet, oval, about ¼ inch long; seeds 10 to 20. Native of Europe and Asia; sometimes escapes from cultivation.

Rose of Sharon *(Hibiscus syriacus)*
A shrub or small tree 3 to 18 feet tall, many-branched. Leaves alternate, simple, 1½ to 4¾ inches long, ¾ to 2½ inches wide, triangular or broadest in the middle, usually more or less 3-lobed; margins with rounded or pointed teeth; upper surface medium green, often shiny, smooth; lower surface paler, smooth. Flowers white, pink, lavender, or rose, with a crimson or purplish blotch at the base, showy, 2 to 4 inches across, emerging solitarily from the leaf axil; petals 5, with wavy margins. Fruit a capsule, persisting into winter, ¾ to 1 inch long, hairy, splitting into 5 parts. Native of Asia; commonly planted as an ornamental shrub; known to spread along roadsides, railroads, thickets and woods.

Autumn olive

Matrimony vine

ALTERNATE, SIMPLE

Rose of Sharon

YUCCAS

Soapweed *(Yucca glauca)*
A short-stemmed shrub to 4 feet tall, with soft wood at the base; young plants lacking a stem. Leaves simple, widely radiating from the base of stem, evergreen, 3 to 16 inches long, ¼ to ½ inch wide, even throughout, stiff, tipped with a spine; margins with white threads that strip and curl; both surfaces gray-green, with a whitish, waxy coating. Flowers greenish-white to white, bell-shaped, drooping, fragrant, 1½ to 2½ inches long, 1 to 1½ inches wide, on an unbranched stalk about 3 feet tall, carrying 25 to 30 flowers and opening from the base upward; petals 6, sharply pointed at the tip. Fruit a cylindrical capsule, 1¾ to 2¾ inches long, ¾ to 2 inches wide, 6-sided, splitting open into 3 parts with 6 columns of black seeds, each about ½ inch wide. Occurs on open, dry, exposed slopes of loess hill prairies of northwestern Missouri. Rare in Missouri.

Arkansas yucca *(Yucca arkansana)*
This yucca is similar to soapweed but differs by having leaves up to 20 inches long, ½ to 1 inch wide, a softer texture, the ends pointed but not tipped with a spine; the petals rounded to bluntly pointed at the tip; and seeds ⅜ inch wide. Occurs on rocky wooded slopes, gravel bars, and banks of streams, on dolomite soils and dolomite glades of southwestern Missouri. Rare in Missouri. (No illustration.)

Spanish bayonet *(Yucca smalliana)*

Escapes from cultivation

A short-stemmed shrub to 6 feet tall, with soft wood at the base; young plants lacking a stem. Leaves simple, widely radiating from the base of stem, evergreen, 6 to 2½ feet long, 1 to 3 inches wide, even throughout, linear, usually straight, tapering to a point, with a short, stout spine at the tip; margins with white threads that strip and curl; both surfaces gray-green, with a whitish, waxy coating. Flowers white, bell-shaped, drooping, fragrant, 2 to 3 inches long, clustered on a branching stalk up to 6 feet tall, carrying 4 to 8 flowers on each branch; petals 6, with pointed tips. Fruit a cylindrical capsule, 1½ to 2½ inches long, ¾ to 1 inch across, hard, 6-sided, splitting open into three parts with six columns of seeds; seeds black, flat, semiglossy, roughly triangular, about ¼ inch wide. Native to the southeastern United States. Commonly cultivated in gardens; occasionally escapes to grow along roadsides, open woods and prairie.

Soapweed

Spanish bayonet

GIANT CANE, PAWPAW

Giant cane *(Arundinaria gigantea)*
Bamboolike canes, woody, branched above, rarely more than 16 feet tall; stems with hollow segments separated by solid joints. Grows in dense colonies due to vegetative spread by rhizomes. Leaves alternate, simple, somewhat crowded at ends of branches, 4 to 12 inches long, ½ to 2½ inches wide, narrowly lance-shaped, tip pointed, base enclosing the stem; margins with small, sharp teeth; leaf blade grasslike with parallel veins. Flowers occur between long intervals, with 5 to 15 flowers clustered on flattened stalks 1½ to 2½ inches long; petals absent. Fruit with furrowed grain, enclosed in flattened spikelets. Occurs in lowlands, along larger streams and at the bases of dolomite cliffs.

Pawpaw *(Asimina triloba)*
A large shrub to small tree up to 30 feet tall, with a slender trunk and broad crown, growing in colonies. Leaves alternate, simple, 6 to 12 inches long, 3 to 5 inches wide, broadest above the middle; margins lacking teeth; upper surface green, smooth; lower surface paler, smooth; emits a disagreeable odor when bruised. Flowers solitary, drooping, about 1 inch across, appearing before the leaves, emitting a winey odor. Fruit banana-shaped, cylindrical, 3 to 5 inches long, yellow when ripe; pulp sweet, edible. Occurs in dense shade on moist lower slopes, in ravines and valleys, along streams and at the bases of wooded bluffs.

ALTERNATE, SIMPLE

Giant cane

Pawpaw

LEAVES ALTERNATE, COMPOUND

ROSES

Prairie rose *(Rosa setigera)*

A shrub with high-climbing, trailing or leaning stems reaching a length of 6 to 15 feet when supported by other shrubs or small trees; in the open, a dense shrub to 4 feet high. Twigs with recurved thorns about ¼ inch long. Leaves alternate, compound, divided into leaflets of 3 on old stems and 3 to 5 on new stems; end leaflet with leaf stalk about ¼ inch long; leaflets 1½ to 4 inches long, about 1 inch wide, lance-shaped to broadest below the middle; margins sharply toothed; upper surface dark green, shiny; lower surface paler, smooth; leaf stalk often with gland-tipped hairs and thorns. Flowers pink, in many-flowered clusters on new stem growth, each flower 1½ to 3¼ inches across; petals pink, about 1½ inches long and wide; stalks with gland-tipped hairs. Fruit red, about ⅜ inch long, fleshy with gland-tipped hairs. Occurs in moist ground and rocky places along streams and spring branches, moist thickets, low open woodlands, pastures, prairie thickets, fencerows and along roadsides.

Pasture rose, Carolina rose *(Rosa carolina)*
A shrub with slender, simple or little-branched stems, attaining a height of 6 inches to 3 feet. Twigs with straight or recurved thorns about ¼ inch long. Leaves alternate, compound, divided into 5 to 7 leaflets each ¾ to 1½ inches long, ¼ to ¾ inch wide, the lower ones smaller, longer than broad; margins coarsely toothed, often fringed with hairs; upper surface dark green, smooth; lower surface paler, a few hairs on the veins. Flowers mostly single, pink, 1½ to 2½ inches across, broadest above the middle; stamens attached to the rim of the hypanthium (upward, cuplike extension of the receptacle); stalks with gland-tipped, bristly hairs. Fruit red, about ¼ inch across, globe-shaped, with scattered gland-tipped hairs. Occurs mainly in dry rocky ground of open woods, glades, prairies, thickets and clearings, and along railroads and roadsides.

Prairie rose

Pasture rose, Carolina rose

ALTERNATE, COMPOUND

ROSES CONT'D

Prairie wild rose *(Rosa arkansana)*
A small shrub with erect stems attaining a height of 1½ feet. Twigs with numerous, straight thorns about ¼ inch long. Leaves alternate, compound, divided into 5 to 9 leaflets, each ½ to 1 inch long, ¼ to ½ inch wide, longer than broad; margins sharply toothed nearly to the base; upper surface dark green, smooth; lower surface paler and soft-hairy. Flowers pink, single or in clusters of 2 to 4, each 1½ to 2¼ inches across; petals ¾ to 1 inch long, broadest above the middle; stamens attached to the rim of the hypanthium (upward, cuplike extension of the receptacle); stalks smooth. Fruit bright red, ½ to ¾ inch broad, smooth, glossy, with tip of fruit with persistent lobes. Occurs in prairies, open banks, loess hills, bluffs, thickets, and along roads and railroads.

Swamp rose *(Rosa palustris)*
A large shrub of swamps or wet ground with erect stems sometimes attaining a height of 8½ feet. Twigs with curved thorns about ¼ inch long. Leaves alternate, compound, divided into 5 to 7 (rarely 9) leaflets, each ¾ to 2½ inches long, lance-shaped to broadest at the middle; margins with numerous fine teeth; upper surface dark green, smooth; lower surface paler, with scattered fine hairs, at least on the veins. Flowers rose-colored, solitary or 2 to 3 flowers in a cluster; petals 5, ½ to ¾ inch long; stamens attached to the rim of the hypanthium (upward, cuplike extension of the receptacle); stalk with rigid, gland-tipped hairs. Fruit red, ¼ to ½ inch broad, globe-shaped, with rigid, gland-tipped hairs or sometimes smooth. Occurs in swamps, low wet woods, borders of upland wooded sinkhole ponds; and along streams, bayous and drainage ditches.

ALTERNATE, COMPOUND

Prairie wild rose

Swamp rose

ROSES CONT'D

Smooth wild rose *(Rosa blanda)*
A straight, upright, colony-forming shrub up to 3 feet tall, usually lacking thorns except at the base. Leaves alternate, compound, divided into 5 to 7 leaflets, each ½ to 1 inch long, ⅜ to ¾ inch wide, broadest at or above the middle; margins toothed; upper surface dull, yellowish-green; lower surface paler, hairy. Flowers pink, often streaked with red, single to few-flowered in clusters; petals 5, about 1 inch long; stamens attached to the rim of the hypanthium (upward, cuplike extension of the receptacle); stalks smooth. Fruit bright red, about ½ inch broad, globe-shaped, smooth. Occurs in open woods, dry hillsides, thickets and roadsides.

Damask rose *(Rosa xdamascena)*
A shrub to 8 feet tall with many hooked thorns along the stems. Leaves alternate, compound, divided into 5 leaflets, each 2½ inches long, egg-shaped; margins smooth; upper surface dark green, smooth; lower surface paler, hairy. Flowers white to pink or red, fragrant; petals 6 to 9; stamens numerous. Fruit rarely developed, which is common among hybrids. The damask rose has been in cultivation since the 16th century and probably long before that. Native of Europe. Occurs around old homesites and fencerows and can escape to roadsides and thickets. Sometimes planted as an "old-fashioned" rose.

Multiflora rose *(Rosa multiflora)*

A diffusely branching shrub up to 12 feet tall, arching or sprawling. Twigs armed with stout, recurved thorns. Leaves alternate, compound, divided into 7 to 9 leaflets, leaflets narrow or broad; margins with numerous sharp teeth; upper surface dark green, smooth; lower surface pale, finely hairy; stalk with a deeply dissected, fringed and comblike stipule (a leaflike growth) along the base of the leaf stalk. Other Missouri roses lack the fringe along the stipule. Flowers white, ¾ to 1½ inches across, in rounded or pyramidal clusters 3 to 6 inches long with 6 to 30 flowers; petals 5; stalks with gland-tipped hairs. Fruit red, ¼ to ⅜ inch long, glossy, smooth, in clusters. Native of Japan; it has escaped in many places to woodlands, along stream banks and in fields and pastures. Designated a state noxious weed.

Smooth wild rose

Damask rose

Multiflora rose

PRICKLY ASH, BRISTLY LOCUST

Prickly ash *(Zanthoxylum americanum)*
A thicket-forming shrub to 8 feet tall, often densely branched above the middle. Twigs have 2 spines at each node, each about ¼ inch long, recurved. Leaves alternate, compound, divided into 5 to 11 leaflets; side leaflets stalkless, end leaflet with short stalk; leaflets aromatic, ¾ to 3 inches long, ⅜ to 1½ inches wide, broadest in the middle; margins entire or with finely rounded teeth; upper surface dull, deep-green, dotted with glands; lower surface paler, hairy on the veins. Flowers yellowish-green, small, appear before the leaves, in clusters with both male and female flowers on the same plant. Fruit green to reddish-brown, in dense clusters, aromatic, splitting to reveal 1 to 2 seeds. Occurs in open rocky woods, along bluffs and in thickets in low moist ground or dry upland.

Bristly locust *(Robinia hispida)*
A shrub 3 to 10 feet tall, spreading by suckering of the roots, the branches numerous, covered by bristly reddish hairs. Leaves alternate, compound, divided into 7 to 15 leaflets, each ¾ to 2 inches long, ¾ to 1¾ inches wide, circular to broadest at or below the middle, tip round to abruptly pointed; margins entire; upper surface light to dark green; lower surface smooth or with occasional scattered hairs. Flowers pink, rose or rose-purple, bonnet-shaped, ¾ to 1¼ inches long, in clusters of 3 to 9; petals 5; stalks bristly-hairy. Fruit a pod, 2 to 3¼ inches long, flattened, with reddish-brown bristles. A native of southeastern United States. Planted as an ornamental and escapes from cultivation.

Escapes from cultivation

Prickly ash

Bristly locust

ALTERNATE, COMPOUND

SUMACS

Smooth sumac *(Rhus glabra)*

A slender-branched shrub to small tree up to 20 feet tall, with a rounded top, forming thickets from root sprouts. Broken leaves, stalks and twigs with white, sticky sap. Leaves alternate, compound, 12 to 16 inches long, with 15 to 23 leaflets; leaflets 2 to 3½ inches long, ½ to 1¼ inches wide, lance-shaped to even throughout, sides unequal; margins coarsely toothed; upper surface dark green, shiny; lower surface paler to conspicuously white, smooth; leaf stalk smooth, lacking leafy wings. Flowers greenish-white, with male and female flowers on separate plants; in large, dense clusters at the end of new growth; petals 5. Fruit red, hairy, about ⅛ inch across, in dense clusters. Occurs in upland prairies, thickets, idle fields, borders, openings of woods, and along roads and railroads.

Winged sumac, shining sumac *(Rhus copallinum)*

A slender-branched shrub to small tree up to 20 feet tall, with a rounded top, forming thickets from root sprouts. Broken leaves, stalks and twigs with white, sticky sap. Leaves alternate, compound, 5 to 12 inches long, with a winged stem and 7 to 17 leaflets; leaflets 1½ to 2½ inches long, ¾ to 1 inch wide, broadest in the middle or even throughout, sides unequal; margins entire to remotely toothed; upper surface dark green, shiny; lower surface paler, hairy. Flowers greenish-white, with male and female flowers on separate plants in large, dense clusters at the end of new growth; petals 5. Fruit red, hairy, about ⅛ inch across, in dense clusters. Occurs in prairies, thickets and open woods; on sandstone, chert and igneous glades; in abandoned fields; and along roads and railroads.

Fragrant sumac *(Rhus aromatica)*

A thicket-forming shrub to 8 feet tall; branches vary from ascending to lying on the ground. Leaves alternate, compound, fragrant, divided into 3 leaflets with the end leaflet ¾ to 1½ inches long, ¾ to 1½ inches wide, on a short stalk about 1 inch long; side leaflets somewhat smaller and stalkless; margins lobed or coarsely toothed, lower edge entire; upper surface dark yellow-green, dull or shiny; lower surface pale, smooth to densely hairy. Flowers yellowish-green, small, in clusters 1½ inches long, ¾ to 1¼ inches wide; petals 5. Fruit red, hairy, about ¼ inch long, in clusters. Occurs in rocky or open woods, thickets, glades and along ledges.

BLACKBERRIES

Pennsylvania blackberry *(Rubus pensilvanicus)*
A shrub with arching canes to 10 feet long, forming open thickets. Stems with broad-based, recurved thorns. Leaves alternate, compound, divided into 3 leaflets on flower stem and 5 leaflets on primary stem; end leaflet on primary stem 3¼ to 4 inches long, 2½ to 3¼ inches wide, broadest at or below the middle, with leaf stalk 1½ to 2 inches long, hairy with few thorns; side leaflets smaller and stalks shorter; flower stem leaflets also smaller; margins irregularly toothed; upper surface slightly hairy; lower surface densely hairy. Flowers white, 1 to 7 in a cluster partially hidden in the leaves attached just below it; 7 to 12 leaflike bracts in the flower cluster; petals 5. Fruit red before ripening to black, glossy, ⅜ to ¾ inch long, juicy, sweet, in clusters. Occurs in rich or rocky wooded hills, thickets, meadows, pastures and prairie openings, and along fencerows and roadsides.

A similar species, highbush blackberry *(Rubus ostryifolius)*, differs by having main flower clusters standing above the leaves attached just below them; fewer leaflike bracts in the flower cluster; the topmost leaflet of the 5 leaflets on the primary stem widest near the middle. Both blackberries share similar habitat and distribution across the state.

Smooth blackberry *(Rubus argutus)*
Usually a low, thicket-forming shrub up to 6 feet tall. Stems with broad-based, recurved thorns. Leaves alternate, compound, with 3 leaflets on the flower stem and 5 leaflets on the primary stem; primary stem upper 3 leaflets 2¼ to 4 inches long, 1½ to 2 inches wide, broadest near the middle; margins densely toothed; upper surface dark green, smooth; lower surface paler, soft-hairy with hooked thorns on the midrib of the end leaflet. Flowers white, about 1 inch across, in clusters of 1 to 7 on short branches of stems; petals 5, narrow, about ⅜ inch across. Fruit black, glossy, juicy, sweet, about ¼ to ¾ inch long. Occurs in low wet woods, thickets, open woods, margins of woods, fencerows, gullies, roadsides and pastures. A similar species, soft-leaved blackberry *(Rubus mollior)*, differs by having short, cylindrical flower clusters on long branches of stems; petals ½ to ¾ inch broad. It occurs in shallow draws in upland thickets and dry open woods in a few scattered counties across southern Missouri.

ALTERNATE, COMPOUND

Pennsylvania blackberry

Smooth blackberry

BLACKBERRIES CONT'D, RASPBERRY

Common blackberry, Allegheny blackberry *(Rubus alleghaniensis)*

An erect shrub up to 8 feet tall, arching high or being supported by surrounding trees or shrubs. Stems with broad-based, recurved or straight thorns about ⅛ inch long. Leaves alternate, compound, with 3 leaflets on the flower stem and 5 leaflets on the primary stem; end leaflet on primary stem 3¼ to 5 inches long, or 2 or 3 times longer than broad, stalked; side leaflets smaller; margins sharply toothed; upper surface dark, dull green, smooth; lower surface paler, hairy. Flowers white, about ¾ inch across, in clusters 4 to 5 inches long, longer than broad, extending beyond the foliage but provided with small leaves at the base; flower stalks with gland-tipped hairs; petals 5. Fruit black, glossy, juicy, sweet, about ¾ inch long. Occurs in rocky open woods and along bluffs, thickets and open valleys. A similar species of blackberry, *Rubus orarius*, differs by having its flower clusters as long as broad, with the flowers mostly crowded at the tip; the topmost leaflet of primary stems broadly egg-shaped to nearly round; scattered throughout the state.

Black raspberry *(Rubus occidentalis)*

An arching shrub, the stems attaining a height of 3 to 7½ feet with tip-rooting stems. Stems with a whitish coating that rubs off; thorns broad-based, recurved. Leaves alternate, compound, with 3 leaflets on the flower stem and 5 leaflets on the primary stem; end leaflet on primary stem 2¾ to 3¼ inches long, broadest below the middle to lance-shaped; side leaflets smaller and narrower; margins densely toothed; upper surface dark green, slightly hairy; lower surface densely white with matted hairs. Flowers white, ½ to ¾ inch across, in clusters of 3 to 7 on the end of shoots; flower stalks bearing stout-hooked thorns; petals 5, narrow. Fruit purple-black, about ½ inch across, aromatic, globe-shaped, juicy, sweet. Occurs in open woods, along bluffs and in thickets. A similar species, red raspberry *(Rubus idaeus)*, differs by having stems that lack a whitish coating; fruit red when ripe; and stalks of flowers and fruits and stems bearing bristles but no thorns. This species occurs on wooded slopes of loess hills in northwestern Missouri and has not been seen in the state in over 20 years.

ALTERNATE, COMPOUND

Common blackberry, Allegheny blackberry

Black raspberry

DEWBERRIES

Dewberry *(Rubus flagellaris)*
A trailing, vinelike plant, the stems up to 10 feet long and armed with recurved thorns. Leaves alternate, compound, with 3 leaflets on the flower stem and 5 leaflets on the primary stem; end leaflet on the primary stem 2¼ to 3¼ inches long, 1¾ to 2½ inches wide, broadest below the middle, the margins coarsely toothed, the upper surface dark green, slightly rough, the lower surface paler, with soft hairs; leaflets on flower stems smaller, the end leaflet on flower stem is broadest near the base. Flowers white, ¾ to 1¼ inch across, in clusters of 1 to 6 flowers that stand well above the foliage; petals 5; flower stalks lack gland-tipped hairs. Fruit red, turning black at maturity, about ¼ inch thick, shiny, juicy, sweet. Occurs in rocky open woods, thickets, prairies and along roadsides and railroad embankments. There are two similar species: The first, upland dewberry *(Rubus invisus)*, has flower stalks with gland-tipped hairs; it is uncommon, occurring in dry rocky woods and on open rocky exposures. The other, one-flowered dewberry *(Rubus enslenii)*, has no gland-tipped hairs, and the end leaflets of the flowering stem are broadly lance-shaped or broadest above the middle; it occurs scattered across the state in old fields, prairies, open banks and along roadsides.

Southern dewberry *(Rubus trivialis)*
A trailing, vinelike plant, the stems up to 3 feet long with more or less evergreen leaflets. The stem has many short, broad-based thorns and reddish gland-tipped hairs. Leaves alternate, compound, with 3 leaflets on the flower stem and 5 leaflets on the primary stem; end leaflet on the primary stem 1¾ to 2¾ inches long, usually twice or more longer than broad, the margins sharply toothed, the upper surface green, shiny, the lower surface dull; leaflets on flowering stem smaller; leaf stalk stout, bearing thorns and often with reddish, gland-tipped hairs. Flowers white to pinkish, ½ to ¾ across, on erect stalks bearing thorns; petals 5. Fruit black, about ¼ to ⅜ inch long, sweet, juicy. Occurs in low or bottomland woods, moist thickets and wooded banks of streams.

Dewberry

Southern dewberry

BLACKBERRY, EASTERN POISON OAK

Himalayan blackberry *(Rubus armeniacus)*
A strong, low-arching bramble, making stems 6 to 9 feet long with the tips sometimes rooting on the ground. Stems with round, broad-based, often recurved thorns about ¼ inch long. Leaves alternate, compound, with 3 leaflets on the flower stem and 5 leaflets on the primary stem; all leaflets are about 3 to 3½ inches long, 2 to 2½ inches wide, oval to broadest below the middle, with a generally narrowing base; margins finely to coarsely toothed; upper surface green, smooth; lower surface with brownish to grayish woolly hairs; leaf stalk hairy with stout thorns. Flowers white or rose, ¾ to 2 inches across, in narrow and long pyramidal clusters; petals 5; flower stalks with densely matted hairs. Fruit black, juicy, about ½ inch thick. Introduced and naturalized along rocky streambeds and banks and in pastures.

Escapes from cultivation

Eastern poison oak *(Toxicodendron pubescens)*
A poisonous, low-branching shrub to 3 feet tall, with leaves divided into 3 leaflets. Leaves alternate, compound, with 3 leaflets; end leaflet 2 to 3½ inches long, 1½ to 2¾ inches wide, leaflet stalk about ¾ inch long, broadest below the middle, symmetrical, the margins with 3 to 4 oaklike lobes, leathery, the upper surface dark green, smooth to hairy, the lower surface paler, densely velvety-hairy; side leaflets smaller, asymmetrical, the leaflet stalk short or absent. Flowers greenish-yellow, about ⅛ inch long, in clusters 1 to 3 inches long; stamens 5, extending beyond the flower. Fruit creamy white, about ¼ inch across, in small, grapelike clusters, hairy when immature, smooth and bearing small, warty projections when ripe. Occurs at edges of dolomite glades and in sandy or rocky open woods; uncommon. Formerly known as *Toxicodendron toxicarium* and earlier as *Rhus toxicodendron*.

ALTERNATE, COMPOUND

Himalayan blackberry

Eastern poison oak

HOP TREE, PRAIRIE ACACIA, DEVIL'S WALKING STICK

Hop tree, wafer ash *(Ptelea trifoliata)*
Usually a rounded shrub, but occasionally a small tree up to 25 feet tall. Leaves alternate, compound, with 3 leaflets; leaflets 4 to 6 inches long, 2 to 4 inches wide, broadest in the middle; margins entire or finely toothed; upper surface dark green, shiny; lower surface paler, slightly hairy; unpleasantly scented. Flowers greenish-white, small; petals 4, somewhat hairy. Fruit in drooping clusters, winged, thin, waferlike, somewhat circular, about ¾ to 1 inch across, unpleasantly scented; seeds about ¼ inch long, reddish-brown. Occurs on limestone and dolomite glades; in prairies, rocky upland woods and low woods; and along fencerows.

Prairie acacia *(Acacia angustissima)*
A shrub rarely more than 2 feet tall. Leaves alternate, compound, divided twice, fernlike, 2 to 5 inches long; leaflets averaging 20 to 33 pairs on a pinna (first division of a compound leaf), end leaflets a pair instead of a single terminal leaflet; leaflets mostly long and narrow, ⅛ to ¼ inch long; both surfaces green, smooth. Flowers greenish-white, about ½ inch across, with 6 to 15 flowers in short globe-shaped clusters; petals 5; stamens 50 to 100 or more. Fruit with solitary pods or in clusters, 2 to 3 inches long, about ¼ inch wide, dark brown, flat, thin. Occurs on dolomite glades, open hillsides and exposed ledges along bluffs.

Devil's walking stick, Hercules' club
(Aralia spinosa)
A spiny, few-branched shrub or slender, flat-topped small tree up to 35 feet tall, often spreading by underground runners. Stem armed with stout, light brown to orange thorns. Leaves alternate, compound, with branches 3 to 4 feet long, 2 to 4 feet wide, armed with small spines and divided into side divisions with numerous leaflets; leaflets with 5 to 6 pairs with an end leaflet, 2 to 3 inches long, 1½ to 2 inches wide, broadest near the base; margins with short-pointed teeth; upper surface dark green, with tiny thorns along the vein; lower surface silvery or gray-green. Flowers light yellow, about ⅛ inch across, in large, branched clusters; petals 5. Fruit black, ¼ inch across, globe-shaped, in large clusters. Occurs on wooded slopes, bluffs and ravines; also in thickets and low to upland sandy woods.

Hop tree, wafer ash

Prairie acacia

Devil's walking stick, Hercules' club

Trumpet creeper

Cross vine

Woolly pipevine

Wisteria

Woody Vines

Yellow honeysuckle

OPPOSITE, SIMPLE

OPPOSITE, COMPOUND

ALTERNATE, SIMPLE

ALTERNATE, COMPOUND

LEAVES OPPOSITE, SIMPLE

HONEYSUCKLES

Yellow honeysuckle *(Lonicera flava)*

A twining or loosely ascending vine. Leaves opposite, simple, the upper pair just below the flowers united at the base to form a disk; both sides of disk totaling about 6 inches across, about 2 inches wide, often longer than broad but sometimes rounded, tips blunt, the upper surface of the disk green or barely whitened; leaves below the disk 2 to 4 inches long, 2 to 3 inches wide, longer than broad or circular, the margins not wavy, the upper surface bright green, smooth, the lower surface grayish-green. Flowers bright orange or yellow, fragrant, ¾ to 1¼ inches long, tube cylindrical, slightly enlarged at the base but not a significant bulge, in clusters arranged in 1 to 3 crowded whorls or layers on a stalk; petals with 2 lips, lower lip narrow, with a solitary lobe, upper lip with 4 lobes. Fruit red to orange-red, globe-shaped, about ¼ inch across in clusters arranged in 1 to 3 crowded whorls or layers on a stalk. Occurs in rocky woods, on ledges and upper slopes above bluffs, and on rocky ground along streams.

Limber honeysuckle, wild honeysuckle *(Lonicera dioica)*

A sprawling or climbing vine, the stems often reaching 10 feet long. Leaves opposite, simple, the upper pair just below the flowers united throughout to form a disk; disk longer than broad, tips abruptly pointed, the upper surface of the disk green or barely whitened; leaves below the disk not united, each 1½ to 3 inches long, 1 to 2 inches wide, the margins often wavy, the upper surface yellowish-green, smooth, the lower surface covered with a white waxy coating. Flowers yellow or greenish-yellow tinged with purple, rose or brick-red; fragrant, ¾ to 1 inch long, tubular with base noticeably enlarged on one side, in clusters arranged in 1 to 3 crowded whorls or layers on a stalk; petals with 2 lips, lower lip narrow, with a solitary lobe, upper lip with 4 lobes. Fruit red, globe-shaped, about ⅜ inch across, in clusters arranged in 1 to 3 crowded whorls or layers on a stalk. Occurs along wooded bluffs and ledges, in upland forests, thickets and rocky banks of streams.

Yellow honeysuckle

Limber honeysuckle, wild honeysuckle

HONEYSUCKLES CONT'D

Grape honeysuckle *(Lonicera reticulata)*
A twining vine to 15 feet, or sometimes somewhat
bushy when no support is present. Leaves opposite,
simple, the upper pair just below the flowers united
throughout to form a disk; both sides of disk totaling
about 6 inches long, 2 inches wide, the disk oval to sometimes
nearly circular, the upper surface with a white coating; leaves
below the disk not united, each 3 to 4 inches long, 1½ to 2½
inches wide, broadly oval to broadest above the middle, the upper
surface dark green to yellow-green, smooth, the lower surface
smooth or somewhat hairy. Flowers pale yellow, fragrant, ¾ to
1 inch long, tubular, noticeably enlarged on one side at the base,
in clusters arranged in 2 to 6 whorls or layers on a stalk; petals
with 2 lips, lower lip narrow, with a solitary lobe, upper lip with 4
lobes. Fruit red to orangish-red, globe-shaped, about ¼ inch across,
in clusters arranged in 2 to 6 whorls or layers on a stalk. Occurs
in open woods, wooded slopes, bluff ledges, upper slopes and
wooded thickets. Also known as *Lonicera prolifera*.

Trumpet honeysuckle *(Lonicera sempervirens)*
A twining vine to 18 feet in length, occasionally
dense. Leaves opposite, simple, the upper pair just
below the flowers united throughout to form a disk;
both sides of disk totaling 2 to 2½ inches long, 1½
to 1¾ inches wide, with each side triangular; leaves below the
disk not united, each 1½ to 3 inches long, 1¼ to 2 inches wide,
oval to broadest above or below the middle, the upper surface
dark yellow-green, semiglossy, smooth, the lower surface smooth.
Flowers deep red on the outside, yellow inside, fragrant, 1½ to 2
inches long, tubular, tip of tube spreading into 5 lobes; in clusters
arranged in 2 to 4 whorls or layers on a stalk. Fruit bright red,
broadest at or below the middle, smooth, in whorls of 2 to 4.
Native to southeastern United States; escaped elsewhere along
roadsides, in open woods, on sandy or rocky stream banks
and in thickets.

Escapes from cultivation

Grape honeysuckle

Trumpet honeysuckle

HONEYSUCKLES CONT'D, CLIMBING DOGBANE

Japanese honeysuckle *(Lonicera japonica)*

A climbing or sprawling vine to 20 feet in length. Leaves opposite, simple, near evergreen, 1 to 3 inches long, ¾ to 1¼ inches wide, egg-shaped or half as wide as long; margins entire, often with fine hairs, or with irregular large teeth or lobes; upper surface dark green, semishiny, hairy; lower surface pale, smooth, hairy along the central vein; none of the leaves joined at the base. Flowers white or pink, turning yellow with age, tubular, hairy, ½ to 1½ inches long, in pairs from leaf axils; petals 2, upper lip with 4 lobes, lower lip with 1 lobe. Fruit black, glossy, smooth, globe-shaped, about ¼ inch long. Native of Asia; escapes from cultivation into thickets, fencerows, edges of woods, open woods, rocky slopes, ditches, roadsides and along railroads.

Climbing dogbane, climbing star-jasmine
(Trachelospermum difforme)

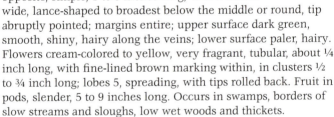

A slender, twining vine, with milky sap, that often dies back to a woody base in winter. Leaves opposite, simple, 1 to 3 inches long, ½ to 2 inches wide, lance-shaped to broadest below the middle or round, tip abruptly pointed; margins entire; upper surface dark green, smooth, shiny, hairy along the veins; lower surface paler, hairy. Flowers cream-colored to yellow, very fragrant, tubular, about ¼ inch long, with fine-lined brown marking within, in clusters ½ to ¾ inch long; lobes 5, spreading, with tips rolled back. Fruit in pods, slender, 5 to 9 inches long. Occurs in swamps, borders of slow streams and sloughs, low wet woods and thickets.

Japanese honeysuckle

Climbing dogbane, climbing star-jasmine

OPPOSITE, SIMPLE

PARTRIDGE BERRY, COMMON PERIWINKLE, WINTERCREEPER

Partridge berry *(Mitchella repens)*

A low-growing, ground-hugging evergreen vine scarcely above the ground and often found trailing over moist, shaded sandstone ledges. Leaves opposite, simple, evergreen, about ¼ to 1 inch in length and width, circular to broadest below the middle; margins entire; upper surface shiny, smooth, often variegated with whitish lines. Flowers white or pinkish, sometimes tinged with purple, very fragrant, about ½ inch long, narrowly trumpet-shaped; petals 4, spreading, densely hairy inside. Fruit red, shiny, about ¼ inch across, globe-shaped, edible but tasteless. Occurs in acid soils along moist ledges of sandstone cliffs, sandy banks of small streams and low, moist, sandy woodlands.

Common periwinkle *(Vinca minor)*

A low-growing, prostrate, mat-forming evergreen vine to a height of 6 inches. Leaves opposite, simple, evergreen, exuding a milky sap when broken, ½ to 1½ inches long, ½ to ¾ inch wide, broadest at or below the middle; margins entire; upper surface dark green, shiny, smooth, central vein light green; lower surface paler, smooth; leaves at the end of twigs often in clusters. Flowers lilac to blue, 1 inch across; petals 5, spreading, tips ending abruptly as if cut off. Fruit a dry capsule, ¾ to 1 inch long, seldom develops on cultivated plants. Native of Europe; commonly planted and sometimes escaping into woods, along rocky banks and in open areas.

Wintercreeper *(Euonymus hederaceus)*

An evergreen vine forming a dense ground cover or climbing or trailing to 20 feet in length. Stems with aerial roots when climbing and when in contact with the ground. Leave opposite, simple, evergreen, about 1½ inches long, ¾ inch wide, broadest at or below the middle; margins irregularly toothed; upper surface green, smooth, leathery in texture, veins light green to cream-colored; lower surface paler, smooth. Flowers greenish-white, about ⅛ inch long, in clusters; petals 4, spreading, margins curved inward, wavy. Fruit a capsule, globe-shaped, orange. Native of Asia; escapes from cultivation into moist to dry woods. Hard to eradicate; seeds spread by birds. Formerly known as *Euonymus fortunei*.

Partridge berry

Common periwinkle

Wintercreeper

LEAVES OPPOSITE, COMPOUND

CROSS VINE, TRUMPET CREEPER

Cross vine *(Bignonia capreolata)*

A vine with foliage persisting through most of winter, climbing as high as 70 feet by forked tendrils. Stem with pith in the shape of a cross when cut crosswise. Leaves opposite, compound, with 2 paired leaflets, 2 to 7 inches long, ¾ to 1½ inches wide, lance-shaped or longer than broad and tapering at both ends; margins entire, wavy; upper surface dark green, smooth to slightly hairy; lower surface paler, veins prominent. Flowers red to orange externally, yellow internally, very showy, about 2 inches long, bell-shaped, in clusters of 2 to 5 flowers; petals 5. Fruit a capsule, 4 to 7 inches long, flattened, leathery, splitting down the sides. Occurs in low bottomland woods, swampy ground, thickets along streams, low fields and fencerows.

Trumpet creeper *(Campsis radicans)*

A vine climbing tall trees or structures by means of aerial rootlets to a height of 60 feet but often seen sprawling over fences or low bushes. Leaves opposite, compound, 8 to 15 inches long; leaflets 7 to 13, ¾ to 3 inches long, ½ to 2 inches wide, broadest below the middle, oval or longer than broad; margins coarsely toothed; upper surface olive-green, shiny, smooth; lower surface paler, smooth; leaflet stalks with wings along the margins, about ¼ inch long. Flowers red to orange on the outside, yellow on the inside, showy, about 2 to 3½ inches long, tubular; lobes 5, spreading. Fruit in pods, 2 to 6 inches long, narrowed toward the ends, splitting open on each side. Occurs in open woods, thickets; on cliffs, stream banks, fallow and old fields; and along roadsides and railroads.

Cross vine

OPPOSITE, COMPOUND

Trumpet creeper

VIRGIN'S BOWER

Virgin's bower *(Clematis virginiana)*
A semiwoody vine climbing to a height of 20 feet by twisting leaf stalks. Leaves opposite, compound, with mainly 3 leaflets, lower sometimes with 5 leaflets; 2 to 3½ inches long, 1½ to 2½ inches wide, thin, broadly rounded; margins entire to deeply toothed or somewhat lobed; upper surface green, slightly hairy; lower surface paler; leaf stalk twists on supports to pull the plant upward. Flowers creamy-white, numerous, ½ to 1¼ inches wide, in clusters; petals absent; sepals 4, ¼ to ½ inch long. Fruit in clusters, with seeds ⅛ inch long and plumelike projections about 1 inch long. Occurs in moist or low ground of woodlands and in thickets bordering streams, ponds and fencerows; especially common on limestone soils. A similar species, sweet autumn clematis (*Clematis terniflora*), differs most noticeably by having 5 leaflets instead of 3. A native of Japan, it escapes from cultivation.

Scattered throughout Missouri

Virgin's bower

OPPOSITE, COMPOUND

LEAVES ALTERNATE, SIMPLE

GRAPES

Frost grape *(Vitis vulpina)*
A vigorous vine climbing high by tendrils to 60 feet in length. Leaves alternate, simple, 4 to 6 inches long, 3 to 6 inches wide, heart-shaped to broadest below the middle or round, base with a broad to narrow U-shaped sinus (cleft between two lobes); margins with prominent teeth, irregular; upper surface dark green, smooth; lower surface paler, with short, straight hairs on the veins and small tufts in the vein axils. Flowers green, minute; male and female flowers in separate clusters on same plant; petals 5, dropping early. Fruit black, glossy, covered with a waxy coating, about ¼ inch thick, turning sweet after frost, in clusters up to 6 inches long. Occurs in bottomland soils along streams in low wet woods, low wooded slopes, bases of bluffs and thickets.

Winter grape *(Vitis cinerea)*
A vine climbing to a height of 50 feet by means of tendrils. Leaves alternate, simple, 4 to 8 inches long or broad, thin, round to heart-shaped, base broadly rounded with a narrow sinus (cleft between two lobes); margins unlobed or with two short lobes, finely to coarsely toothed; upper surface dark green, with a few cobwebby hairs; lower surface covered with white to gray, cobwebby and straight hairs. Flowers green, minute; male and female flowers in separate clusters on same plant; petals 5, dropping early. Fruit black, about ¼ inch thick, bitter until late autumn, in clusters 3 to 6 inches long. Occurs in low woods and alluvial soils along streams, in thickets and in fencerows.

Frost grape

Winter grape

GRAPES CONT'D

Summer grape *(Vitis aestivalis)*
A vigorous vine climbing to a height of 35 feet by means of tendrils, or sprawling over low bushes and trees. Leaves alternate, simple, 2 to 8 inches long and wide, heart-shaped or round; margins of some irregularly toothed and unlobed, some leaves with margins shallowly to deeply 3- to 5-lobed, lobe sinuses (cleft between two lobes) narrow and rounded, base heart-shaped; upper surface yellowish-green with a few hairs on the veins; lower surface whitish, with light rusty, cobwebby hairs. Flowers green, minute; male and female flowers in separate clusters on same plant; petals 5, dropping early. Fruit dark blue to black, ¼ to ½ inch thick, with a thin whitish coating, sweet, juicy, in clusters 3 to 5 inches long. Occurs in dry, rocky, upland woods; thickets and glades; and along rocky slopes.

Riverbank grape *(Vitis riparia)*
A vine climbing to 75 feet by means of tendrils. Leaves alternate, simple, 4 to 6 inches long, 3½ to 5 inches wide, broadest below the middle to round, with two short side lobes, base rounded with a broad sinus (cleft between two lobes); margins coarsely toothed, lined with fine hairs; upper surface yellowish-green, smooth; lower surface paler, hairy on the veins and in the vein axils. Flowers yellowish-green, minute; male and female flowers in separate clusters on same plant; petals 5, dropping early. Fruit purple to blue with a white, waxy coating, about ⅜ inch thick, sweet, in clusters 2 to 5 inches long. Occurs in low woods, thickets and banks of streams in bottomland soils.

Summer grape

Riverbank grape

GRAPES CONT'D

Red grape *(Vitis palmata)*
An attractive, high-climbing, slender, delicate vine named for the color of its branches. Leaves alternate, simple, 2¾ to 4¾ inches long and broad, heart-shaped or oval in outline, base narrowly U-shaped; margins with 3 to 5 prominent lobes, teeth irregular; upper surface dark green, glossy; lower surface much paler green. Flowers yellowish-green, minute; male and female flowers in separate clusters on same plant; petals 5, dropping early. Fruit bluish-black, about ¼ inch thick, sweet. Occurs in sloughs and low wet woods.

Raccoon grape *(Ampelopsis cordata)*
A vine climbing by tendrils to a length of 60 feet; the most aggressive native vine in the state, capable of smothering small- to medium-sized trees. Leaves alternate, simple, 2 to 5 inches long, 2½ to 4½ inches wide, triangular, base flattened; margins coarsely toothed; upper surface olive-green, rather dull, smooth; lower surface paler, smooth or with a few scattered white hairs, especially on the veins. Flowers greenish, small, in flat-topped loose clusters; petals 5. Fruit ¼ inch across, globe-shaped, changing color as they develop from green to orange to rose-purple and finally to turquoise blue. Occurs in bottomland soils in valleys, low woods, slopes near streams and along fencerows.

Red grape

Raccoon grape

SUPPLE-JACK, WOOLLY PIPEVINE

Supple-jack *(Berchemia scandens)*
A high-climbing, large, woody, twining vine in bottomland forests; a smaller, densely matted, sprawling vine on dolomite glades; tendrils absent. Leaves alternate, simple, 1½ to 3 inches long, ¾ to 1½ inches wide, broadest below the middle to longer than broad and tapering at both ends; margins wavy or slightly toothed; upper surface dark green, shiny, leathery, smooth; lower surface with side veins conspicuous, nearly straight, evenly spaced and parallel. Flowers greenish-yellow, small, in loose clusters at the ends of stems; petals 5. Fruit bluish-black, about ¼ inch long, slightly flattened, fleshy. Occurs in low swampy woods in the southeastern lowlands; on dolomite glades and rocky dolomite ledges; along bluffs; or in rocky ground along streams and small draws of ravines in Ozark counties.

Woolly pipevine, Dutchman's pipe
(Aristolochia tomentosa)
A twining, high-climbing vine to 75 feet; tendrils absent. Leaves alternate, simple, 3 to 6 inches long, 2 to 3½ inches wide, heart-shaped, base heart-shaped; margins entire; upper surface dark green, somewhat densely hairy with matted wool; lower surface pale, densely hairy with matted wool; leaf stalk densely hairy with matted wool. Flowers yellow or greenish-yellow with dark purple at the base of the center, 1 to 2 inches long, flower tube sharply curved, shaped somewhat like a Dutch pipe; calyx (outer part of flower) with 3 lobes; petals absent; smells of rotting flesh, attracting flies and gnats for pollination. Fruit a dry capsule, 1½ to 3 inches long, 1 to 1¼ inches wide, cylindrical, grayish-brown, hanging, 6-sided with many seeds. Occurs in low wooded bottomlands along streams, often along stream banks, usually climbing trees or brush; rarely found in open ground.

Supple-jack

Woolly pipevine,
Dutchman's pipe

ALTERNATE, SIMPLE

CATBRIERS

Catbrier *(Smilax bona-nox)*
A stout, spiny vine with angled branches, either low-climbing or extensively climbing to a height of 25 feet; tendrils present. Leaves alternate, simple, 1½ to 4½ inches long, ¾ to 4 inches wide, heart-shaped, broadest below the middle, triangular, or sometimes fiddle-shaped; margins entire or set with stiff thorns; upper surface green, smooth, often with white blotches; lower surface paler, usually with a few thorns on the midvein. Flowers yellowish-green, small, with male and female flower clusters on the same plant, clusters with 3 to 20 flowers; petals 6. Fruit black, ¼ inch thick, globe-shaped, in clusters. Occurs in rocky open woods, low ground in valleys and along streams, dolomite glades, thickets and fields.

Greenbrier *(Smilax glauca)*
A slender, spiny vine climbing by coiled tendrils. Leaves alternate, simple, 1½ to 4 inches long, 1 ¼ to 3 inches wide, broadly heart-shaped, oval or lance-shaped; margins entire; upper surface dark green, sometimes with lighter blotches; lower surface smooth, conspicuously whitened with a waxy coating or bluish-gray or silvery. Flowers yellowish-green, small; male and female flower clusters on the same plant; clusters with 6 to 12 flowers; petals 6. Fruit black, ¼ inch thick, globe-shaped, shiny, with a white waxy coating. Occurs in acid soils of chert, sandstone or igneous origin in rocky woodlands, wooded valleys and moist ground along streams, open grown fields, and along fencerows and roadsides.

Catbrier

Greenbrier

CATBRIERS CONT'D, LADIES' EARDROPS

Bristly greenbrier *(Smilax hispida)*
A stout vine with bristlelike black spines, climbing high by tendrils to a length of 40 feet. Leaves alternate, simple, 2 to 6 inches long, 2 to 5½ inches wide, oval, broadest below the middle, heart-shaped, to lance-shaped; margins entire but sometimes minutely toothed; upper surface green, smooth, shiny, with the 5 to 7 main veins sunken; lower surface paler, smooth. Flowers yellowish-green, small, with male and female flower clusters on the same plant, in clusters of 5 to 26 flowers; cluster stalks much longer than the leaf stalks; petals 6. Fruit bluish-black, lacking a whitish coat, about ¼ inch thick, globe-shaped; cluster stalks much longer than the leaf stalks. Occurs in low woods in valleys and thickets, along stream banks and on rich wooded slopes.

Round-leaved catbrier *(Smilax rotundifolia)*
A climbing vine to 20 feet long with tendrils and stout spines, sometimes forming tangled thickets. Leaves alternate, simple, 2 to 6 inches long, 1 to 6 inches wide, from broadest below the middle to circular or heart-shaped; margins entire or occasionally with scattered teeth; upper surface dark green, smooth; lower surface slightly paler, smooth. Flowers greenish-yellow, small, with male and female flower clusters on the same plant, in clusters; petals 6. Fruit bluish-black, covered with a grayish-blue coating, about ¼ inch thick. Occurs in mostly bottomland soils along streams or in valleys, and in wet woodlands and thickets.

Ladies' eardrops *(Brunnichia ovata)*
A tendril-climbing woody vine to 40 feet, with green to reddish-brown stems. Leaves alternate, simple, 1¼ to 6 inches long, ½ to 3 inches wide, thin, broadest below the middle to lance-shaped; margins entire; upper surface light green, smooth; lower surface smooth or slightly hairy. Flowers greenish, small, in clusters 2 to 10 inches long at the end of stems; petals absent; sepals are petal-like, 5-parted. Fruit pink, showy, ¾ to 1½ inches long, drooping, resembling ear pendants, hence the common name. Occurs in swamps, low wet woods and moist bottomland thickets. Formerly known as *Brunnichia cirrhosa*.

Bristly greenbrier

Round-leaved catbrier

Ladies' eardrops

BITTERSWEETS

American bittersweet *(Celastrus scandens)*
A twining woody vine, climbing to heights of 20 feet but more commonly found sprawling on bushes or fences. Leaves alternate, simple, 2 to 4 inches long, 1 to 2 inches wide, broadest below the middle to oval to lance-shaped; margins entire or with small, finely pointed teeth; upper surface dark yellowish-green, smooth; lower surface paler, smooth. Flowers greenish-white to yellow, small; male and female flowers in clusters usually on separate plants; petals 5. Fruit orange to red, about ¼ inch across, globe-shaped, in clusters, splitting into 3 sections, each section with 1 to 2 globe-shaped seeds; seeds covered with a bright red, fleshy coating, persistent and showy in autumn. Occurs in woodlands, on rocky slopes, along bluffs, in borders of glades, in thickets and along fencerows.

Oriental bittersweet
(Celastrus orbiculatus)
A twining woody vine climbing to heights of 20 feet but more commonly found sprawling on bushes or fences. Leaves alternate, simple, 2 to 4 inches long and wide, circular to broadest above the middle; margins with small, rounded teeth; upper surface green, smooth; lower surface paler, smooth. Flowers greenish, small; male and female flowers in clusters usually on separate plants; petals 5. Fruit orange-yellow to orange, about ¼ inch across, globe-shaped, splitting into 3 sections, each section with 1 to 2 globe-shaped seeds; seeds covered by a red coating. Native to Asia; escapes from cultivation. The fruits are not as showy as the native American bittersweet.

American bittersweet

Oriental bittersweet

MOONSEEDS, CUPSEED

Moonseed *(Menispermum canadense)*

A twining vine to 25 feet high, climbing or sprawling; tendrils absent. Leaves alternate, simple, 2 to 6 inches long and wide, with 3 to 7 lobes; point of leaf stalk attachment not at the leaf margins but just inside on the lower surface of the leaf; margins entire; upper surface dull green, smooth; lower surface much paler green, pale gray or silvery gray. Flowers greenish-white to white, small, numerous; petals 4 to 8; stamens numerous. Fruit dark blue to black with a whitish coating that can be rubbed off, about ¼ inch across, in grapelike clusters; seeds circular, shaped like a crescent moon. Occurs in low moist woods and thickets in ravines and along streams, in valleys, along fencerows and at the bases of bluffs.

Carolina moonseed, Carolina snailseed
(Cocculus carolinus)

A slender, twining vine to 40 feet high; tendrils absent. Leaves alternate, simple, 2 to 4 inches long and wide, broadest below the middle to triangular; margins entire or 3- to 5-lobed; upper surface dark green, smooth or with scattered hairs; lower surface paler, densely hairy; leaf stalk sharply bent near the blade. Flowers yellowish-green, small; petals 6. Fruit brilliant red, glossy, smooth, about ¼ inch across, flattened, in grapelike clusters; seeds with a spiral pattern, snail-like. Occurs in rocky open woods, dolomite and limestone glades, bottomlands bordering streams and ponds, fencerows and roadsides.

Cupseed *(Calycocarpum lyonii)*

A twining vine to 30 feet that dies back to the ground in severe winters. Leaves alternate, simple, 3 to 8 inches long, 3 to 7 inches wide, rounded to broadest below the middle; margins with 3 to 5 deep lobes with rounded sinuses (the space between lobes); upper surface dark yellow-green, smooth; lower surface slightly paler, with scattered long, straight hairs on the veins. Flowers white, small; petals absent. Fruit black, about ¾ inch across, in grapelike clusters; seed in the shape of a hollow bowl or cup, with a keel on the round side. Occurs in moist soils in wooded valleys and along banks of streams, in thickets and in borders of fields.

Moonseed

Carolina moonseed, Carolina snailseed

Cupseed

LEAVES ALTERNATE, COMPOUND

VIRGINIA CREEPER, WOODBINE, PEPPER VINE

Virginia creeper, woodbine
(Parthenocissus quinquefolia)
A vine climbing to a height of 75 feet with many-branched tendrils having sucker disks and aerial roots. Leaves alternate, compound, with 5 leaflets (rarely 7) or sometimes 3 leaflets on new growth; leaflets 2 to 6 inches long, 1 to 3 inches wide, broadest at or below the middle; margins coarsely toothed, except near the base; upper surface dark green, dull, smooth; lower surface paler green, smooth. Flowers greenish, small, 25 to 200 per cluster; petals 5. Fruit dark purple, about ¼ inch across, globe-shaped, in clusters 3 to 6 inches long, 1½ to 2½ inches wide; stalk red. Occurs in open and moist woods, fencerows, rocky wooded hillsides, ravines and bluffs.

Woodbine *(Parthenocissus vitacea)*
A vine climbing by tendrils usually without sucker disks to a height of 30 feet, typically found sprawling over bushes and rocks; tendrils few-branched. Leaves alternate, compound, with 5 leaflets on new growth; leaflets 2½ to 4 inches long, 1½ to 2½ inches wide; margins coarsely toothed; upper surface green, glossy; lower surface paler, net-veined, smooth, the veins sometimes hairy. Flowers yellowish-green, small, 10 to 60 per cluster; petals 5. Fruit bluish-black, about ⅜ inch across, globe-shaped, in somewhat flat-topped clusters, 3 to 6 inches long; stalk red. Occurs in rich woods and stream banks; rarely found. Also known as *Parthenocissus inserta*.

Pepper vine *(Ampelopsis arborea)*
A rather slender, upright vine, either high-climbing or bushy, tendrils present or absent. Leaves alternate, compound, with 9 to 34 leaflets; leaflets ½ to 1½ inches long, broadest below the middle; margins coarsely toothed to deeply lobed; upper surface dark green, shiny, smooth; lower surface lighter green, smooth, or with a few scattered white hairs especially along the veins. Flowers greenish-white, small, in clusters ¾ to 2½ inches across; petals 5. Fruit first green, then pink or bluish to shiny black at maturity, about ¼ inch long, with warty dots, in clusters. Occurs along wooded banks of streams and river forest floodplains and at the bases of bluffs along streams.

Virginia creeper, woodbine

Woodbine

Pepper vine

POISON IVY, MARINE VINE

Poison ivy *(Toxicodendron radicans)*
A poisonous vine up to 60 feet high, trailing or climbing by aerial roots, or a low, upright shrub. Leaves alternate, compound, with 3 leaflets variable in size and shape; end leaflet 1¼ to 8 inches long, ½ to 5 inches wide, stalk ½ to 1¾ inches long; side leaflets with unequal sides, 1¼ to 6¾ inches long, ½ to 4 inches wide, stalk about ⅛ inch long; margins largely toothed or lobed; upper surface dull green, smooth; lower surface paler, somewhat hairy. Flowers greenish-white, small, fragrant, in clusters 1 to 4 inches long; petals 5. Fruit creamy-white, waxy, about ¼ inch across, globe-shaped, indented slightly at the tip, in persistent, grapelike clusters. Occurs in floodplain and upland forests on level and sloping ground, bottomland soils along streams, in thickets and along fencerows, roadsides and railroads. Formerly known as *Rhus radicans*.

Marine vine *(Cissus trifoliata)*
A climbing or trailing vine to 30 feet high, climbing by tendrils. Leaves alternate, compound, very fleshy or succulent, with 3 leaflets or leaves deeply 3-lobed; bad-smelling when crushed; end leaflet 1½ to 2 inches long, 1¼ to 2 inches wide, fan-shaped, commonly 2-lobed; margins coarsely toothed; both surfaces dull green, smooth or with a few minute white hairs. Flowers greenish, small, 50 to 80 in the umbrella-shaped cluster; petals 4. Fruit black, shiny, about ¼ inch long, on curved stalks ½ to 1 inch long, in clusters. Occurs along upper portions of south- or west-facing rocky ledges of dolomite bluffs and upper slopes of dolomite bluffs bordering streams. Formerly known as *Cissus incisa*. Classified as state rare.

ALTERNATE, COMPOUND

Poison ivy

Marine vine

WISTERIA

Wisteria *(Wisteria frutescens)*
A twining, woody vine reaching a length of 40 feet, tendrils absent. Leaves alternate, compound, 5 to 12 inches long, with 5 to 11 leaflets; leaflets ¾ to 2½ inches long, ½ to 1 inch wide, broadest at or below the middle to lance-shaped; margins entire; upper surface dull green to partly shiny, smooth; lower surface paler, bearing white hairs, especially along the veins. Flowers from white to blue to lilac or purple, very fragrant, several, in hanging clusters 8 to 12 inches long, 1½ to 2 inches wide; petals 5, in the typical pea-flower configuration. Fruit in narrow pods 2 to 5 inches long, with large, black, shiny seeds. Occurs in low wet or swampy woods and along the borders of swamps, sloughs and slow streams. A similar species, Chinese wisteria *(Wisteria sinensis)*, differs by having 7 to 13 leaflets; another, Japanese wisteria *(Wisteria floribunda)*, has 13 to 19 leaflets. Both species have flower clusters that are twice as long as the native wisteria and more loosely arranged. The non-natives are aggressive and not recommended for planting.

ALTERNATE, COMPOUND

Wisteria

Non-native shrubs and woody vines naturalized in Missouri

Shrubs

Autumn olive	*Elaeagnus umbellata*
Border privet	*Ligustrum obtusifolium*
Bristly locust*	*Robinia hispida*
Bush honeysuckle	*Lonicera maackii*
Common barberry	*Berberis vulgaris*
Common buckthorn	*Rhamnus cathartica*
Damask rose	*Rosa xdamascena*
Himalaya berry	*Rubus procerus*
Japanese barberry	*Berberis thunbergii*
Matrimony vine	*Lycium barbarum*
Bush honeysuckle	*Lonicera X bella*
Multiflora rose	*Rosa multiflora*
Peach	*Prunus persica*
Perfumed cherry	*Prunus mahaleb*
Rose of Sharon	*Hibiscus syriacus*
Spanish bayonet*	*Yucca smalliana*
Sweet mock orange	*Philadelphus coronarius*
Himalayan blackberry	*Rubus armeniacus*

Woody vines

Chinese wisteria	*Wisteria sinensis*
Common periwinkle	*Vinca minor*
Japanese honeysuckle	*Lonicera japonica*
Japanese wisteria	*Wisteria floribunda*
Oriental bittersweet	*Celastrus orbiculatus*
Trumpet honeysuckle*	*Lonicera sempervirens*
Sweet autumn clematis	*Clematis terniflora*
Wintercreeper	*Euonymus hederaceus*

*Native southeast of Missouri

Index

Acacia
　Prairie, 106
Acacia angustissima, 106
Aesculus
　glabra, 32
　pavia, 32
Alder, 62
Allegheny blackberry, 100
Alnus serrulata, 62
Alternate-leaved dogwood, 76
Amelanchier arborea, 76
American barberry, 62
American bittersweet, 134
American black currant, 66
American bladdernut, 36
American Christmas mistletoe, 28
American hornbeam, 64
American hydrangea, 26
American plum, 40
American smoke tree, 78
Amorpha
　canescens, 36
　fruticosa, 36
Ampelopsis
　arborea, 138
　cordata, 126
Andrachne phyllanthoides, 74
Aralia spinosa, 106
Aristolochia tomentosa, 128
Arkansas yucca, 84
Aronia melanocarpa, 44
Arrowwood
　Downy, 16
　Northern, 18
　Ozark, 18
　Softleaf, 18
　Southern, 18
Arundinaria gigantea, 86
Ascyrum hypericoides, 28
Ash
　Prickly, 94
　Wafer, 106
Asimina triloba, 86

Autumn clematis, sweet, 120, 144
Autumn olive, 82, 144
Azalea, wild, 70

Barberry
　American, 62
　Common, 62, 144
　Japanese, 62, 144
Bayonet, Spanish, 84
Beautyberry, 26
Berberis
　canadensis, 62
　thunbergii, 62, 144
　vulgaris, 62, 144
Berchemia scandens, 128
Bignonia capreolata, 118
Big tree plum, 42
Bittersweet
　American, 134
　Oriental, 134, 144
Blackberry, 100
　Allegheny, 100
　Common, 100
　Highbush, 98
　Himalayan, 104, 144
　Pennsylvania, 98
　Smooth, 98
　Soft-leaved, 98
Black chokeberry, 44
Black currant, American, 66
Blackhaw, 16
　Rusty, 16
　Southern, 16
Black huckleberry, 54
Black raspberry, 100
Bladdernut, American, 36
Blueberry
　Highbush, 52
　Lowbush, 52
Border privet, 30, 144
Bristly greenbrier, 132

Bristly locust, 94, 144
Brunnichia
    cirrhosa, 132
    ovata, 132
Buckbrush (*Andrachne* sp.), 74
Buckbrush (*Symphoricarpos* sp.), 24
Buckeye
    Ohio, 32
    Red, 32
Buckthorn
    Carolina, 56
    Common, 30, 144
    Lance-leaved, 56
    Southern, 58
    Woolly, 58
Bumelia, gum, 58
Bumelia
    lanuginosa, 58
    lycioides, 58
Burning bush, 22
Bush honeysuckle, 30, 144
Buttonbush, 20

Callicarpa americana, 26
Calycocarpum lyonii, 136
Campsis radicans, 118
Cane, giant, 86
Carolina buckthorn, 56
Carolina moonseed, 136
Carolina rose, 88
Carolina snailseed, 136
Carolina willow, 46
Carpinus caroliniana, 64
Catbrier, 130
    Round-leaved, 132
Ceanothus
    americanus, 74
    herbaceus, 74
    ovatus, 74
Celastrus
    orbiculatus, 134, 144
    scandens, 134
Celtis tenuifolia, 78

Cephalanthus occidentalis, 20
Cercis canadensis, 76
Cherry
    Choke, 42
    Perfumed, 44, 144
Chestnut oak, dwarf, 78
Chickasaw plum, 40
Chinese wisteria, 142, 144
Chionanthus virginicus, 20
Chittim wood, 58
Chokeberry, black, 44
Choke cherry, 42
Cissus
    incisa, 140
    trifoliata, 140
Clematis, sweet autumn, 120, 144
Clematis
    terniflora, 120, 144
    virginiana, 120
Climbing dogbane, 114
Climbing star-jasmine, 114
Cocculus carolinus, 136
Common barberry, 62, 144
Common blackberry, 100
Common buckthorn, 30, 144
Common elderberry, 34
Common periwinkle, 116, 144
Coral berry, 24
Corkwood, 72
Cornus
    alternifolia, 76
    amomum ssp. *obliqua*, 12
    drummondii, 12
    florida, 12
    foemina, 14
    foemina ssp. *foemina*, 14
    foemina ssp. *racemosa*, 14
    obliqua, 12
    racemosa, 14
Corylus americana, 64
Cotinus obovatus, 78
Crab apple
    Narrow-leaved, 38
    Prairie, 38
    Sweet, 38

Crataegus
    pruinosa, 60
    uniflora, 60
Cross vine, 118
Cupseed, 136
Currant
    Golden, 68
    American black, 66

Damask rose, 92, 144
Deciduous holly, 54
Deerberry, 52
Devil's walking stick, 106
Dewberry, 102
    One-flowered, 102
    Southern, 102
    Upland, 102
Dirca palustris, 58
Dogbane, climbing, 114
Dogwood
    Alternate-leaved, 76
    Flowering, 12
    Gray, 14
    Pagoda, 76
    Rough-leaved, 12
    Silky, 12
    Stiff, 14
    Swamp, 12
Downy arrowwood, 16
Dutchman's pipe, 128
Dwarf chestnut oak, 78
Dwarf hackberry, 78

Eardrops, ladies', 132
Eastern poison oak, 104
Eastern redbud, 76
Eastern witch-hazel, 70
Elaeagnus umbellata, 82, 144
Elderberry
    Common, 34
    Red-berried, 34
Elm, water, 56
Euonymus, winged, 22

Euonymus
    alatus, 22
    americanus, 22
    atropurpureus, 22
    fortunei, 116, 144
    hederaceus, 116
    obovatus, 24

False indigo, 35
Farkleberry, 52
Flowering dogwood, 12
Forestiera acuminata, 14
Fragrant sumac, 96
French mulberry, 26
Fringe tree, 20
Frost grape, 122
Frosty hawthorn, 60

Gaylussacia baccata, 54
Giant cane, 86
Goat willow, 50
Golden currant, 68
Gooseberry
    Missouri, 66
    Prickly, 66
    Wild, 66
Goose plum, wild, 40
Grape
    Frost, 122
    Muscadine, 126
    Raccoon, 126
    Red, 126
    Riverbank, 124
    Summer, 124
    Winter, 122
Grape honeysuckle, 112
Gray dogwood, 14
Greenbrier, 130
Greenbrier, bristly, 132
Gum bumelia, 58

Hackberry, dwarf, 78
Hamamelis
    vernalis, 70
    virginiana, 70

Hardhack, 50
Haw
    Black, 16
    Possum, 54
    Rusty black, 16
Hawthorn
    Frosty, 60
    One-flowered, 60
Hazel
    Eastern witch, 70
    Ozark witch, 70
Hazelnut, 64
Hercules' club, 106
Hibiscus syriacus, 82, 144
Highbush blackberry, 98
Highbush blueberry, 52
Highbush huckleberry, 52
Himalaya berry, 104, 144
Himalayan blackberry, 104, 144
Holly, deciduous, 54
Honeysuckle
    Bush, 30, 144
    Grape, 112
    Japanese, 114, 144
    Limber, 110
    Trumpet, 112, 144
    Wild, 110
    Yellow, 110
Hop hornbeam, 64
Hop tree, 106
Hornbeam
    American, 64
    Hop, 64
Hortulan plum, 42
Huckleberry
    Black, 54
    Highbush, 52
Hydrangea, American, 26
Hydrangea arborescens, 26
Hypericum
    hypericoides, 28
    lobocarpum, 28
    prolificum, 28
    spathulatum, 28

Ilex
    decidua, 54
    verticillata, 54
Indigo, false, 36
Indigo bush, 36
Ironwood, 64
Itea virginica, 72

Japanese barberry, 62, 144
Japanese honeysuckle, 114, 144
Japanese wisteria, 142, 144
Jointweed, 80

Ladies' eardrops, 132
Lance-leaved buckthorn, 56
Lead plant, 36
Leatherwood, 58
Leitneria floridana, 72
Ligustrum obtusifolium, 30, 144
Limber honeysuckle, 110
Lindera
    benzoin, 68
    melissifolia, 68
Locust, bristly, 94, 144
Lonicera
    × *bella*, 30
    dioica, 110
    flava, 110
    japonica, 114, 144
    maackii, 30, 144
    prolifera, 112
    reticulata, 112
    sempervirens, 112, 144
Lowbush blueberry, 52
Lycium barbarum, 82, 144
Lyonia mariana, 80

Maiden-bush, 74
Malus
    angustifolia, 38
    coronaria, 38
    ioensis, 38
Marine vine, 140
Matrimony vine, 82, 144

Meadowsweet, 50
Meadow willow, 48
Menispermum canadense, 136
Missouri gooseberry, 66
Missouri willow, 46
Mistletoe, American Christmas, 28
Mitchella repens, 116
Mock orange, 26
    Sweet, 26, 144
Moonseed, 136
    Carolina, 136
Mulberry, French, 26
Multiflora rose, 92, 144
Muscadine, 126
Musclewood, 64

Nannyberry, 20
Narrow-leaved crab apple, 38
Neviusia alabamensis, 60
New Jersey tea, 74
Ninebark, 80
Northern arrowwood, 18

Oak
    Dwarf chestnut, 78
    Poison, 104
Ohio buckeye, 32
Olive, autumn, 82, 144
One-flowered dewberry, 102
One-flowered hawthorn, 60
Orange, mock, 26
Oriental bittersweet, 134, 144
Ostrya virginiana, 64
Ozark arrowwood, 18
Ozark witch-hazel, 70

Pagoda dogwood, 76
Parthenocissus
    inserta, 138
    quinquefolia, 138
    vitacea, 138
Partridge berry, 116
Pasture rose, 88
Pawpaw, 86

Peach, 44, 144
Pennsylvania blackberry, 98
Pepper vine, 138
Perfumed cherry, 44, 144
Periwinkle, common, 116, 144
Philadelphus
    coronarius, 26, 144
    pubescens, 26
Phoradendron leucarpum, 28
Physocarpus opulifolius, 80
Pipevine, woolly, 128
Planera aquatica, 56
Plum
    American, 40
    Big tree, 42
    Chickasaw, 40
    Hortulan, 42
    Wild, 40
    Wild goose, 40
Poison ivy, 140
Poison oak, Eastern, 104
Polygonella americana, 80
Pondberry, 68
Possum haw, 54
Prairie acacia, 106
Prairie crab apple, 38
Prairie rose, 88
Prairie wild rose, 90
Prairie willow, 48
Prickly ash, 94
Prickly gooseberry, 66
Privet
    Border, 30, 144
    Swamp, 14
Prunus
    americana, 40
    angustifolia, 40
    hortulana, 42
    mahaleb, 44, 144
    mexicana, 42
    munsoniana, 40
    persica, 44, 144
    virginiana, 42

Ptelea trifoliata, 106
Pussy willow, 50

Quercus prinoides, 78

Raccoon grape, 126
Raspberry
    Black, 100
    Red, 100
Red-berried elderberry, 34
Red buckeye, 32
Redbud, 76
Red grape, 126
Red raspberry, 100
Redroot, 74
Rhamnus
    caroliniana, 56
    cathartica, 30, 144
    lanceolata, 56
Rhododendron
    prinophyllum, 70
    roseum, 70
Rhus
    aromatica, 96
    copallinum, 96
    glabra, 96
    radicans, 140
    toxicodendron, 104
Ribes
    americanum, 66
    cynosbati, 66
    missouriense, 66
    odoratum, 68
Riverbank grape, 124
Robinia hispida, 94, 144
Rosa
    arkansana, 90
    blanda, 92
    carolina, 88
    xdamascena, 92, 144
    multiflora, 92, 144
    palustris, 90
    setigera, 88

Rose
    Carolina, 88
    Damask, 92, 144
    Multiflora, 92, 144
    Pasture, 88
    Prairie, 88
    Prairie wild, 90
    Smooth wild, 92
    Swamp, 90
Rose of Sharon, 82, 144
Rough-leaved dogwood, 12
Round-leaved catbrier, 132
Rubus
    allegheniensis, 100
    argutus, 98
    armeniacus, 104, 144
    enslenii, 102
    flagellaris, 102
    idaeus, 100
    invisus, 102
    mollior, 98
    occidentalis, 100
    orarius, 100
    ostryifolius, 98
    pensilvanicus, 98
    procerus, 104, 144
    trivialis, 102
Running strawberry bush, 24
Rusty black haw, 16

Salix
    caprea, 50
    caroliniana, 46
    discolor, 50
    eriocephala, 46
    exigua, 46
    gracilis var. *textoris*, 48
    humilis, 48
    interior, 46
    petiolaris, 48
    sericea, 48

Sambucus
   canadensis, 34
   pubens, 34
   racemosa ssp. *pubens*, 34
Sandbar willow, 46
Service berry, 76
Shadbush, 76
Sharon, rose of, 82, 144
Shining sumac, 96
Shrubby St. John's-wort, 28
Sideroxylon
   lanuginosum, 58
   lycioides, 58
Silky dogwood, 12
Silky willow, 48
Smilax
   bona-nox, 130
   glauca, 130
   hispida, 132
   rotundifolia, 132
Smoke tree, American 78
Smooth blackberry, 98
Smooth sumac, 96
Smooth wild rose, 92
Snailseed, Carolina, 136
Snowbell, 72
Snow wreath, 60
Soapweed, 84
Softleaf arrowwood, 18
Soft-leaved blackberry, 98
Southern arrowwood, 18
Southern blackhaw, 16
Southern buckthorn, 58
Southern dewberry, 102
Spice bush, 68
Spanish bayonet, 84, 144
Spiraea
   alba var. *alba*, 50
   tomentosa, 50
Staggerbush, 80
St. Andrew's cross, 28
Staphylea trifolia, 36
Star-jasmine, climbing, 114

Steeple bush, 50
Stiff dogwood, 14
St. John's-wort, 28
   Shrubby, 28
Strawberry bush, 22
   Running, 24
Styrax americanum, 72
Sumac
   Fragrant, 96
   Shining, 96
   Smooth, 96
   Winged, 96
Summer grape, 124
Supple-jack, 128
Swamp dogwood, 12
Swamp privet, 14
Swamp rose, 90
Sweet autumn clematis, 120, 144
Sweet crab apple, 38
Sweet mock orange, 26, 144
Sweet-spire, 72
Symphoricarpos
   occidentalis, 24
   orbiculatus, 24

Tea, New Jersey, 74
Toxicodendron
   pubescens, 104
   radicans, 140
   toxicarium, 104
Trachelospermum difforme, 114
Trumpet creeper, 118
Trumpet honeysuckle, 112, 144

Upland dewberry, 102

Vaccinium
   arboreum, 52
   pallidum, 52
   stamineum, 52
   vacillans, 52

Viburnum
   dentatum, 18
   lentago, 20
   molle, 18
   ozarkense, 18
   prunifolium, 16
   rafinesquianum, 16
   recognitum, 18
   rufidulum, 16
Vinca minor, 116, 144
Virginia creeper, 138
Virginia willow, 72
Virgin's bower, 120
Vitis
   aestivalis, 124
   cinerea, 122
   palmata, 126
   riparia, 124
   rotundifolia, 126
   rupestris, 126
   vulpina, 122

Wafer ash, 106
Wahoo, 22
Ward's willow, 46
Water elm, 56
Wild azalea, 70
Wild gooseberry, 66
Wild goose plum, 40
Wild honeysuckle, 110
Wild plum, 40
Willow
   Carolina, 46
   Goat, 50
   Meadow, 48
   Missouri, 46
   Prairie, 48
   Pussy, 50
   Sandbar, 46
   Silky, 48
   Virginia, 72
   Ward's, 46

Winged euonymus, 22
Winged sumac, 96
Winterberry, 54
Wintercreeper, 116, 144
Winter grape, 122
Wisteria, 142
   Chinese, 142, 144
   Japanese, 142, 144
Wisteria
   floribunda, 142, 144
   frutescens, 142
   sinensis, 142, 144
Witch-hazel
   Eastern, 70
   Ozark, 70
Wolfberry, 24
Woodbine, 138
Woolly buckthorn, 58
Woolly pipevine, 128

Yellow honeysuckle, 110
Yucca, Arkansas, 84
Yucca
   arkansana, 84
   glauca, 84
   smalliana, 84, 144

Zanthoxylum americanum, 94

Visit

MDC's Online Field Guide
for More Info

mdc.mo.gov/field-guide

Want to know more about Missouri's plants, animals, and mushrooms? Visit our mobile-friendly online field guide. It's packed with information, images, and links to help you identify and learn more about Missouri's natural history. Use any digital device to access the field guide at home or outdoors. Find out what to look for right now, or search species accounts to identify your latest finds. Compare similar species, scan mammal tracks, find good places to see the plants and animals you're interested in, and even share photos. Visit *mdc.mo.gov/field-guide* and start exploring!

Raccoon grape

Spice bush

Mock orange

American bittersweet